T0287186

Israelis and Palestinians

With love to Vivette, Daniel, David, Ruth, Helen, Sam, Josie and Bill, each with either Jewish or Muslim heritage or both.

Israelis and Palestinians

From the Cycle of Violence to the Conversation of Mankind

Jonathan Glover

polity

First published in 2024 by Polity Press

Polity Press
65 Bridge Street
Cambridge CB2 1UR, UK

Polity Press
111 River Street
Hoboken, NJ 07030, USA

ISBN-13: 978-1-5095-5978-7

A catalogue record for this book is available from the British Library.

Library of Congress Control Number: 2023939908

Typeset in 10.5 on 12pt Sabon
by Fakenham Prepress Solutions, Fakenham, Norfolk NR21 8NL

For further information on Polity, visit our website:
politybooks.com

CONTENTS

Contents

FIGURES

ACKNOWLEDGEMENTS

I am grateful for helpful comments on drafts or discussions of the book's issues: to Rosa Barugh and to her friends in Ramallah, and to Paul Cartledge, Giulia Cavaliere, Martin Elton, Sam Glover, David Heyd, Milly Heyd, Daniel Jowell, Wendy Kristianasen, Jeff McMahan, Maren Meinhardt, Paul Menzel, Edward Mortimer, Daniel Nerenberg, Derek Osborn, Alex Reid, Marian Roberts, Bonnie Steinbock, Paul Troop, Dan Wikler and Noam Zohar. I have learnt from all of them.

Ian Malcolm has been both a wonderful editor of this book and its eloquent friend. I am grateful to an extent only he and I understand.

George Szmukler over several years has generously given much time to reading and discussing this book. I have gratefully adopted many of his suggestions. I hope he will forgive me for retaining the pictures, against his (perhaps better) judgement.

Alan Ryan has been a source of stimulus since, as young Fellows of New College, Oxford, we and our families shared a house in London. He has not grown less stimulating. His comments in our conversations greatly improved the book.

Richard Keshen made constructive comments, as he has done on all my books since he was a graduate student. As this may be my last book, it is the place to thank him for an adult life of friendship and collaboration, including many phone calls between Canada and England. Conversations with Richard have hugely enriched my work.

My life with Vivette has been, among so many other things, a continuing conversation. She has shaped the way I think and feel for more than half a century. She probably doesn't realize how much her outlook has, through seeping into mine, made this book (and my life) so much better than they would have been.

Thanks are due for the following permissions:

Scripture quotations are taken from The Authorized (King James) Version. Rights in the Authorized Version in the United Kingdom are vested in the Crown. Reproduced by permission of the Crown's patentee, Cambridge University Press.

Extracts from 'The Owl's Night', 'I belong there' and 'A Rhyme for the Odes' by Mahmoud Darwish are taken from *Unfortunately, it was Paradise: Selected Poems* (2003) and used with permission of University of California Press; permission conveyed through Copyright Clearance Center, Inc.

Excerpts from Dror Moreh, *The Gatekeepers* are reprinted with permission from Skyhorse Publishing.

Quotes from Julia Bacha's documentary *Budrus* are reproduced courtesy of Just Vision.

Extract from *Aubade* by W.H. Auden, Copyright © 1974 by W.H. Auden. Reprinted by permission of Curtis Brown, Ltd. All rights reserved.

Excerpts from *Beowulf*, Copyright © 2000 by Seamus Heaney. Reproduced by permission of Faber and Faber Ltd. and from BEOWULF, translated by Seamus Heaney. Copyright © 2000 by Seamus Heaney. Used by permission of W.W. Norton & Company, Inc.

Extract from speech by Winston Churchill in London, July 1941, reproduced with permission of Curtis Brown, London on behalf of The Estate of Winston S. Churchill © The Estate of Winston S. Churchill.

Extract from statement by Osama Bin Laden, from *Messages to the World: The Statements of Osama Bin Laden*, Bruce Lockhart (ed.), James Howarth (trans.). Verso (2005), reproduced with permission of The Licensor through PLSclear.

Extract from Yigal Amir, after killing Yitzhak Rabin, taken from *Killing a King: The Assassination of Yitzhak Rabin and the Remaking of Israel* by Dan Ephron. Copyright © 2015 by Dan Ephron. Used by permission of W.W. Norton & Company, Inc.

Extract from *The End of Days* by Gershom Gorenberg. Copyright © 2000 by Gershom Gorenberg. Reproduced with permission of Oxford University Press through PLSclear, and courtesy of Gersholm Gorenberg.

Extract from *What Is a Palestinian State Worth?* by Sari Nusseibeh, Cambridge, Mass.: Harvard University Press. Copyright © 2011 by the President and Fellows of Harvard College. Used by permission. All rights reserved.

Extract from 'The Place Where We are Right' by Yehuda Amichai, used with permission of University of California Press, from *The Selected Poetry of Yehuda Amichai*, Yehuda Amichai, (1996); permission conveyed through Copyright Clearance Center, Inc.

Paul Celan, excerpt from 'Death Fugue', translated by Michael Hamburger, from *Poems of Paul Celan*. Copyright © 1972, 1980, 1988, 1995 by Michael Hamburger. Reprinted with the permission of the publishers, Persea Books, Inc. (New York), www.perseabooks.com. All rights reserved, and reprinted by kind permission of Carcanet Press, Manchester, UK.

Extract from *To the Taliban* by Shukria Rezaei reproduced by kind permission of Shukria Rezaei.

PROLOGUE
AFTER 7 OCTOBER 2023

The incursion itself surprised even Israeli Intelligence. But the real shock, felt round the world, came from the *degree* of violence: the killing (including civilians, children and babies) and the taking of hostages (including children). Many rightly said it should be called by its name: not a military attack but terrorism. But even most terrorist acts seem moderate in comparison.

This book, on the verge of printing when Hamas attacked, was written in search of a deeper understanding of the long-running Israel–Palestine conflict. It gives reasons for seeing several deep fault-lines in human psychology as central to creating and sustaining the conflict. Some of them were strikingly visible in October 2023 and after.

One fault-line is the willingness to commit with fanatical rigidity to poorly founded (often false) beliefs. This can turn people with rival claims or different views into enemies, making it hard to agree on compromises for peace.

Another relevant fault-line is often found in a group whose members share a common identity. This identity may be rooted in a nation, a religion or a shared history. Hostility to other groups, especially towards those who have harmed or humiliated 'our' group, seems close to a human universal. Retaliation, vengeance, retribution, backlash, revenge, getting even, teaching them a lesson: the words and phrases vary, but they reflect much the same psychology. It is at the heart of cycles of violence, especially long and bitter ones like the Israeli–Palestinian one.

It may seem redundant to think and talk at this abstract level about a particular real-world conflict. Aren't these 'fault-lines' just platitudes? Isn't it obvious to most of us that many people are easily persuaded of dubious beliefs, that groups resent humiliations or defeats and often try to avenge them?

Of course, fault-lines *can* be described in platitudinous generalities. Bur this book was written to look in detail at how they help create and promote the Israel–Palestine cycle of violence. There is no magic to remove this psychology. But seeing its terrible influence clearly may help to loosen its grip on us.

Rigid Commitment to Poorly Based Beliefs

The terror attacks of 7 October were extreme by any measure. And they had an extra horror. The ideology behind it was a Nazi one.

The section on Gaza in this book describes the Nazi influence. The Hamas Constitution explicitly endorsed the fraudulent antisemitic document *The Protocols of the Elders of Zion*. It claimed to be an account of Jewish plans for world domination. The account in the chapter on Gaza includes Goebbels' conversation with Hitler about the *Protocols*. Both accepted the document as genuine. Hitler said the only solution was extermination of the Jews. That year the extermination camp furnaces were expanded to enable more Jewish men, women and children to be murdered.

At least since 1989, Hamas knew all this but did not delete their Constitution's endorsement of the *Protocols*. Many years later, a Hamas spokesperson, when asked about this, said "We need time to adjust".

Backlash

A leader of any nation that had suffered a staggeringly huge atrocity would express their people's grief and rage. Probably most would express determination to punish the attackers and to deter any repetition. Prime Minister Netanyahu did so in his speech declaring war: '*What happened today is unprecedented in Israel and I will see to it that it doesn't happen again … The IDF will immediately use all its strength to destroy Hamas's capabilities.*' At this point in the speech decent people can agree.

But at other points he expressed more passionate sentiments: Israel will 'take mighty vengeance', and 'the enemy will pay an unprecedented price'. This book centres around a sustained argument against backlash, which is at the heart of any continuing cycle of violence.

Some parts of this backlash are appalling in themselves. The international law of war requires combatants to take great care not to harm civilians. The Israeli retaliation started with massive bombing of heavily populated Gaza. It would be absurd to suggest that only members of Hamas had their homes destroyed or lost their lives. Netanyahu did make a token gesture. He advised civilians not involved with Hamas to avoid the bombing by going away. But where were they to go? Where, if they existed, were the safe places?

Bombing was only part of the indiscriminate punishment. The Israeli government cut off Gaza's water, food, fuel and power. Did they think that only Hamas supporters would die of thirst, starvation or cold? When the power to hospitals gives out, do only Hamas patients die?

The indiscriminate retaliation cannot be justified. But, psychologically, it is an understandable response. Leaders and many ordinary citizens, reeling from appalling atrocities directed at them, may care less about harm to bystanders than about 'getting even'. There are many awful actions that can be understood. But that does not stop them from being indefensible.

As well as these strong ethical objections to such backlash, there is its sheer irrationality. The aim of 'teaching them a lesson' is to prevent them from doing such an atrocity again. But, in the context of a cycle of violence, groups who are victims of backlash are far more likely to think about how they in turn can hit back.

The leader of Hamas is Ismail Haniyeh. In 1948, his parents were driven out from their village. The family only returned to Gaza after the Oslo Agreement. In the interim of more than half a century, Ismail Haniyeh was born and spent his childhood in a refugee camp. His adult commitment to Hamas is not a surprise. Ismail Haniyeh was not alone. When he was an infant, Abdul Rantisi's parents were forced to flee to the Gaza strip. When he was nine, Israelis killed his uncle. His unsurprising adult commitment to Hamas included planning suicide bombings.

When each side uses violent backlash to teach the other a lesson, nobody learns anything. The backlash is central to keeping the cycle of violence going. One factor is moving from thinking of others as people to thinking in abstractions. 'They' are terrorists or cruel occupiers; communists or fascists; unbelievers or religious fanatics. Seeing others in these ways makes people harder and more cruel. Everybody loses.

Most of us have some disposition towards vengeance, retribution, 'getting even'. In personal life even those of us who don't believe in it may feel its pull when someone is horrible to a person we care about. Yet avengers in private life are less likely to end up happy than to end up disgraced or in prison. And around the world cycles of violence ruin the lives of so many on both sides.

Could Better Understanding of the Conflict Help Weaken It?

Clear thinking requires separating the dispute over land from the resulting cycle of violence. Homeland claims, while sometimes theological, are mainly historical. 'We lived here before you drove us out by force' versus 'We lived here and were driven out long before you'. These ownership claims are hard (perhaps impossible?) rationally to adjudicate.

War, even undeclared, creates a dark psychology. Cycles of violence take on a life of their own.

We do not have to take sides. My sympathy is with both peoples, tragically entwined over the same homeland. Sympathy, but also dismay at this dark time as some on each side push it ever further away.

Theorists of violent conflict rightly seek rational causes, looking for carrots and sticks to influence decisions. But peace-making needs to go psychologically deeper, often into irrational areas. Thucydides, on the causes of the Peloponnesian war, did not stress rational plans, but fear. *I consider the truest cause, though one least openly stated, to be this: the Athenians were becoming powerful and inspired fear in the Spartans and forced them into war.* Thomas Hobbes, his first English translator (and a careful observer of the English Civil War) followed him in this. Fearing others' growing power can be rational, but resulting decisions can be irrational. As can 'getting even' in a cycle of violence.

How can we humans be so stupid? Our partly emotion-driven actions will often escape the control of our intellect. The twentieth-century Italian revolutionary Antonio Gramsci was jailed by Mussolini's fascists. Seeing his cause's poor chances of success, his favourite quote was 'Pessimism of the intellect, optimism of the will'. Roughly: when, rationally, things look dark, stay committed, don't leave the battle, and your cause just may win.

Sometimes things look *very* dark, as now in Israel–Palestine. Then, the passions of the will may urge us: 'Keep on fighting for the cause. If they hit us, hit them back'. But perhaps we should listen to the soft voice of the intellect: 'But that way we all lose'.

PART ONE
THE CYCLE OF VIOLENCE

1

DISPUTED HOMELAND

The Israel–Palestine conflict is one of the world's most intractable. Some say it goes back to 1948 when the State of Israel was recognized by the United Nations. Others say it goes back to the early twentieth century. Others point to nineteenth-century roots. Some push it back as far as the destruction of the Temple in Roman times. This competition over dates is not important, though the history is. What really matters is trying to help reduce the conflict. This chapter starts with three of its related central features: exile, land and home.

I: Exile

In the Israel–Palestine conflict much on both sides is coloured by exile. Jewish experience of this goes back to biblical times: *By the waters of Babylon, there we sat down, yea, we wept, when we remembered Zion. We hanged our harps upon the willows in the midst thereof. For there they that carried us away captive required of us a song; and they that wasted us required of us mirth, saying, Sing us one of the songs of Zion. How shall we sing the Lord's song in a strange land?*[1]

Long after biblical times, Jews experienced rejection and murder for many centuries before the Nazi genocide.

The Palestinians do not have that history, but they have never had self-government, and their exile is recent and current. Many were driven by Israeli force from their homes in towns and villages into a stateless limbo. Mourid Barghouti described the impact of this. *It stretches before me, as touchable as a scorpion, a bird, a well; visible as a field of chalk, as the prints of shoes. It is a land, like any land. We sing for it only so that we may remember the humiliation of having it taken from us. Our song is not for some sacred thing of the past but for our current self-respect that is violated anew every day by the occupation.*[2]

Those staying in Israel find that state moving towards one where Jews have protected national identity but Palestinians do not.

Palestinians and Exile: Two Memories

Ghada Karmi was a child when her family fled Jerusalem, fearing massacre as at Deir Yassin, where survivors told of mutilation, rape and murder of pregnant women.

Twenty of the men were ... paraded in triumph around the streets of the Jewish areas of Jerusalem. They were then brought back and shot directly over the quarries ... into which their bodies were thrown. The surviving villagers fled in terror, and the empty village was then occupied by Jewish forces. The worst of it was that the gangs who had carried out the killings boasted about what they had done and threatened publicly to do so again. They said it had been a major success in clearing the Arabs out of their towns and villages. ... We never set eyes on Fatima or our dog or the city we had known ever again ... our hasty, untidy exit from Jerusalem was no way to have said goodbye to our home, our country and all that we knew and loved.[3]

Mourid Barghouti reflected on his brother's exile: *Take me to the home of Hajja Umm Isma'il, to houses I have lived in and paths I have trodden. Here you are: treading them again – as Mounif could not, Mounif, who lies now in his grave on the edge of Amman. Being forbidden to return killed him. Three years ago they sent him back from the bridge after a day of waiting. He tried again a few months later and they sent him back a second time. My mother, three years after the event, cannot forget her last moments with him on the bridge. He was desperate to get back to the Palestine that he had left when he was just eighteen years old ... His sudden death was the great deafening collapse in the lives of the whole family. He had arrived at this final gate but it had not opened for him.*[4]

Israelis and Exile: Two Memories

On the night when the United Nations had voted to recognize Israel, Amos Oz's father whispered in the dark to him about being humiliated by other children at his school in Vilna. Amos Oz's grandfather went to complain. The bullies attacked him too in the playground, forcing him to the ground and removing his trousers: *the girls laughed and made dirty jokes, saying the Jews were all so-and-sos, while the teachers watched and did nothing, or maybe they were laughing too.* Amos Oz's father went on: *from now on, from the moment we have our own state, you will never be bullied just because you are a Jew and because Jews are so-and-sos. Not that. Never again. From tonight that's finished here. For ever.* Amos Oz sleepily reached out to touch his father's face, but *instead of his glasses my fingers met tears.*[5]

David Grossman remembered silence. *My generation, the children of the early 1950s in Israel, lived in a thick and densely populated silence. In my neighbourhood, people screamed every night from their nightmares ... when we walked into a room where adults were telling stories of the war, the conversation would stop at once.* Daily on the radio for ten minutes they read names of people seeking relatives lost in Europe. *Every lunch of my childhood was spent listening to the sounds of this quiet lament.* The Eichmann trial brought another loss: *of something deeper, which we did not understand at the time and which is still being deciphered throughout the course of our lives. Perhaps what we lost was the illusion of our parents' power to protect us from the terrors of life. Or perhaps we lost our faith in the possibility that we, the Jews, would ever lead a complete, secure life. And perhaps, above all, we felt the loss of the natural, childlike faith – faith in man, in his kindness, in his compassion.*[6]

Shared Themes

Palestinians know what they have lost. This must be bound up with despair. Israel, with huge financial and military support from the United States, is a regional superpower. The chances of its defeat by its Arab neighbours are extremely small. Despair mixed with a sense of injustice is a recipe for bitterness.

Many centuries of antisemitism make Israelis reluctant to trust their security to others. The effects of the Nazi genocide go down the generations. Those who lose faith that Jews can ever lead a complete secure life, or in human kindness and compassion, may well lack the trust needed for peace. Nightmare happenings in nearby countries must feed fears of what might happen to them if Israel relaxed its bristling toughness. For many the dread behind the toughness must be huge.

Few are pleased by reminders that experience of exile is common to both sides. Jewish Israelis rightly say that the Palestinian experience is nowhere near what the Nazis did to Jews. Palestinians ask why they should have been forced out because of what others did. But there are shared themes. Ghada Karmi's parents kept the departure from the children. David Grossman's family fell silent when the children came in. These adults might have understood each other. Mourid Barghouti wrote that Palestinians sang about their homeland only to *remember the humiliation of having had it taken from us.* This might have been understood by Jewish exiles in ancient Babylon hanging up their harps on the willows. Barghouti's song is also *for our current self-respect that is violated anew every day by the Occupation.* Violated self-respect is something Amos Oz's family also knew.

II: Land

Some Israelis say their ownership of the land comes from 70 CE, when the Romans under Titus destroyed Jerusalem and exiled

the Jews. The claim has been doubted. *Did* the huge Jewish
diaspora come from that expulsion? Shlomo Sand says the
Romans never deported whole peoples, and that *Galut*, now
translated as 'exile', often referred to subjugation. He argues
that emigration by an inland agricultural people does not easily
explain the many thriving Jewish Mediterranean communities.
The trickle of emigrating Jews *could not have grown into
hundreds of thousands, let alone millions.* Sand's own account
of the numbers cites large-scale conversions. After the Persian
defeat by Alexander the Great, Mediterranean culture became
less tribal and Judaism became less exclusive. Some conquered
peoples were forced to adopt Judaism. Converted Gentiles
led to 7 or 8 per cent in the Roman Empire being Jews. Sand
(whose own views have been disputed by geneticists) says that,
without this impact of Greek universalism, there would be
about as many Jews as Samaritans.[7]

It is hard to see where truth lies on this. But how much
hangs on it? If Sand is right, does an important part of Israel's
claim to the land collapse? Or, putting the same question
another way, if the ancestors of modern Jews *were* exiled
from their land by the Romans, would this support a modern
claim to own the land?

As a thought experiment, imagine a family in England
who farm a piece of land they have owned for generations.
A Danish family arrives, having impressive evidence that,
before the Norman Conquest, *their* ancestors owned the land
until the Normans drove them out and took it. The reluctant
English family come, rightly, to accept the evidence. Should
they hand over the land to the Danish family?

Should the earlier claim trump the later one? Current
legal thinking suggests not. The English ancestors legally
bought ownership, which includes the right to pass on
their property. Unlike renting, ownership brings security.
Trumping by unexpected historical claims would make *all*
current ownership (a little bit) less secure. Many legal
systems avoid insecure ownership by giving priority to
current owners. Descendants of Native Canadians driven off
their land have a case for compensation. But do they really
own the land under Toronto?

Is it different when the issue is not between individuals
but between peoples? In Poland the borders of the country

expanded and contracted at different times. People in a Polish town or village could be a mixture of Poles, Jews, Russians, Germans, Ruthenians and others. Ethnic groups' historical trumping rights could create a chaos of litigation, perhaps violence. The Middle East is more like Poland than rural England.

Before World War II, Hitler demanded the Sudetenland from Czechoslovakia. He incorporated Austria into Germany. The post-war settlement undid this and redrew boundaries east of Germany. But it was understood that, in the interests of peace, despite some questionable boundaries, European countries should not make territorial claims against each other. In Europe this was largely observed – until Putin attacked Ukraine. The ban reflects something that underlies rejection of 'ancient ownership' claims. It is not that later claims are more just. It is pragmatic, rooted in the values of peace and stability. Conquest has been frequent, so peace depends on time limits on claims to reverse it. UN Resolution 242 bans the acquisition of territory by war. In most cases this applies only to wars since 1945. This tells against Israeli claims to the occupied territories. It reflects the value of peace and stability. But Israel, whose state was recognized after 1945, over seventy years ago, can appeal to stability in rejecting Palestinian claims against its UN-recognized boundaries.

Concern for the lives and security of people on both sides suggests basing peace on something humanly more important than the shifting sands of legal ownership claims, whether ancient or more recent.

III: Home

To trigger a cycle of violence between nations, defeats and humiliations have to be *felt*. People must have a sense of belonging to the nation and care what happens to it. Since the 1980s historians and social scientists have changed our understanding of this key element of nationalism.[8] Ernest Gellner argued that industrial society led to European nation-states replacing the medieval 'unity of Christendom'. He denied that nationalism was an ancient latent force, saying it is really a product of industrial society, that needs skills only transmitted by an education system backed by a state. For him, nations are not inscribed into the nature of things.[9]

Benedict Anderson saw this account needs supplementing. Nation-states are too big for everyone to know each other. Some way is needed to create a sense of nationhood, a 'we'. He suggested that 'nation' should be defined as *an imagined political community – and imagined as both inherently limited and sovereign. It is imagined because the members of even the smallest nation will never know most of their fellow-members, meet them, or even hear of them, yet in the minds of each lives the image of their communion.* In Europe, printing presses let national languages replace Latin in mass communication. This let many people *think about themselves in profoundly new ways. They could form an 'imagined community'*, with a shared national self-image. National consciousness depends on this created 'we'.[10]

Nations are not inscribed in the nature of things? Gellner mixed truth and overstatement. For him, European nation-*states* came from industrial society. But *nations* did exist earlier. Stateless nations include the Kurds, the Jews before Israel and the Palestinians now. Not any 'we' counts as a nation. (We parachutists? We atheists? A family?) A national 'we' has to share some (not all) features. These include ethnicity, language, religion and culture. Herodotus quotes Athenians calming Spartan worries that they would make peace with the powerful 'barbarians', by citing things they shared. *We are all of us Greeks, of one blood and one tongue, united by the temples that we have raised to the gods, and by the way in which we offer them sacrifice, and by the customs that we have in common. For the Athenians to prove traitors to all of this would be a terrible thing.*[11]

Critics of Israeli or Palestinian claims to the land attack their *national* component. Against the Israeli claim: 'Most of you do not descend from the Jews when the Temple was destroyed'. Against the Palestinian claim: 'You were just some Arabs on the land, not a Palestinian nation'. The facts are debatable. An imagined community is a capacious thing. We should respect how peoples think of who they are. The hope must be for a more or less just peace between the two nations as they imagine themselves.

Homeland Israel

In 1898, Theodor Herzl, the grandfather of Zionism, staked the Jewish claim: *On this land, where so little grows now, ideas for all of mankind have grown, and it is because of this that no-one can deny that there is an indelible link between us and this land – if there ever existed any legal claim to any territory on this earth.*[12]

Long before political theorists, nationalist politicians saw nations as imagined communities. They showed each other ways to stir national imagination. Herzl took from Bismarck ideas for creating an imagined community. *Believe me, the politics of a whole people – particularly if it is scattered all over the world – can only be made with imponderables that hover high in the air. Do you know out of what the German Empire arose? Out of dreams, songs, fantasies and black-red-gold ribbons.* Herzl thought Bismarck understood the *stirrings, mysterious and undeniable like life itself, which rose out of the unfathomable depths of the folk-soul in response to the dream.*[13]

Zionists needed to foster an imagined community. More important than coloured ribbons were dreams, songs and fantasies. Whatever the historical truth, the story of the diaspora exiled from Jerusalem is a unifying theme in the imagined community of hugely many Jews. Many times they will have said 'Next year in Jerusalem'. Very many of them will have suffered their share of not at all imagined perse-cution. Ancient ownership may not give modern property rights. But a more subtle claim, coming from the hopes and imagined community of a scattered and often persecuted people, need not be a weak one. Especially after the Nazis, this one became strong. It is for a land and home of their own.

After so much persecution in other states, perhaps only a state of their own could provide enough refuge. But none of this included the right to drive out another people. For peoples without states, the need to reconcile these last two sentences is the deep problem. It often looks both impossible and essential to solve.

Amos Oz

Countries, like some other homes, can arouse conflicting emotions. In an interview with Jonathan Freedland, Amos Oz said: *I love Israel, but I don't like it very much. I love it because of the argumentativeness, because every staircase in Israel is full of memories and stories and conflicting ideas.*[14]

Victor and Eva Klemperer

One current sadness of the Nazi genocide is that many people, thinking they know all about it, react as to a tired cliché. The murder of around six million Jews by the Nazis is not news. Refugee Jews reaching Israel had escaped, although nearly all will have lost people close to them. Virtually all will have experienced kinds of Nazi persecution that now are less remembered. Because Israel was created to provide a national home for Jews, it is worth looking at what a hostile state could do to the sense of home of Jewish citizens who escaped murder.

Victor Klemperer was a scholar of French literature, an enthusiast of Voltaire and Montesquieu. As a Jew in the time of Hitler he lost his academic post in Dresden. He still worked on his book on *The Century of Voltaire and Rousseau.* His wife, Eva, was a concert pianist and painter. They had to take cleaning jobs. Victor cashed some insurance to buy a second-hand car. Eva found walking hard. Taxis were expensive. The car had unreliable starting and huge fuel consumption. But they came to like it. *The driving is gradually becoming more enjoyable … the starter works, I am driving better, and we use the car a lot – Eva really has become more mobile … Motorized wedding anniversary … it was a great pleasure … the car really provided what we had so much hoped it would … And today we want to go to Rochlitz. Car, car over all. It has taken a terrible hold of us, d'une passion devorante.*

It was not to last. In 1938 Heinrich Himmler cancelled all Jewish driving licenses.

Despite poor health, Eva loved to garden. The couple had a house converted for them in Dolzschen, a village outside Dresden. *The little house is now a proper house, in fact a 'villa'. The large hallway is very elegant, even more elegant is*

Figure 1: Victor and Eva Klemperer
© SLUB Dresden/Deutsche Fotothek/Unknown photographer

the '*winter garden*'. Victor recorded buying *Eva's longed-for trees and bushes.*

In December 1939, Victor went to pay his tax, and to hand over their clothes coupons, now denied to Jews, The Party official surprised him: 'You must leave your house by the 1st of April'. They could sell or rent it, but for living they were entitled only to a room in the Jewish house. (Possibly two rooms, as Eva was 'Aryan'.) Victor saw *the difficulties we shall face, without anyone at all benefiting as a result – the sadistic machine simply rolls over us.* It would be worse for Eva. *Her house, her garden, her activity.* And Eva loved their cat, who had nearly all their meat ration. For the cat *our moving out will be a death sentence.* The move was chaos. *I am virtually ravaging my past. Whole piles of books ... have been removed ... all the reviews of my work 1904–33 ... We are both most deeply depressed ... It destroys our future ... Principal activity of this day, burning, burning, burning for hours on end.* Later diary entries were headed with the address of the Jews' House at 15B Caspar David Friedrich Strasse. *There are many moments in the day when one would wish to be dead and buried.* There was a bedroom and a living room, with a public hallway between them. *So our whole lifestyle has been transformed. But it is still quite impossible to know whether a tolerable existence can be established here ... The first thing I found waiting for me was a letter from the Jewish Community: personal details for the Labour Service: to all Jews from sixteen to sixty. If I am enlisted for digging, my heart will be the death of me.*[15]

Leaving aside the almost unimaginable scale of the Nazi mass murder, the Klemperers' story gives strong support to the case for a Jewish state. Victor should not have lost his job. He should not have been stopped from driving. They should not have lost their clothes ration. Victor should not have been banned as a Jew from the library reading room. Nor should the books he wrote have been removed from the lending room. Nor should Jews have been subject to the humiliation of the early evening curfew.

Absolutely central was the loss of their home. Germany once had seemed a particularly civilized country towards Jews. If antisemitism even there could boil up to the point where a couple's home was not secure, shouldn't Jews have the option of living in their own state? Herzl wrote: *In countries where we have lived for centuries we are still cried down as strangers ... The majority may decide which are the strangers; for this, as indeed every point which arises in the relations between nations, is a question of might.*[16] (Victor

Klemperer, admiring the French Enlightenment, disliked nationalism including Zionism. I am hoping his ghost would forgive me using his diary to illustrate Herzl's point.)

Homeland Palestine

In 1901 Israel Zangwill had coined the phrase: *Palestine is a country without a people, the Jews are a people without a country.* In 1969 this was echoed by then Israeli Prime Minister Golda Meir: *There was no such thing as Palestinians. It is not as though there was a Palestinian people in Palestine considering itself as a Palestinian people and we came and threw them out and took their country away from them. They did not exist.*[17] But they did. Many in the Israeli forces noticed them: *The commander on the spot was Yitzhak Rabin. He recalled how Ben-Gurion had first called him into his office to discuss the fate of both Lydd and Ramla: Yigal Alon asked: what is to be done with the population? Ben Gurion waved his hand in a gesture that said: 'Drive them out!'.*[18]

Mahmoud Darwish saw the contrast. *The refugees scattered by Nazism found a homeland for themselves in Palestine, and the refugees driven out by Zionism, where are they to live? Where?*[19]

The Palestinian imagined community was rooted in the land where they lived and a perceived threat to their lives there. But the idea of their national identity was not taken up in the outside world as the idea of Jewish national identity was. In the 1917 Balfour Declaration, the British Foreign Secretary Arthur Balfour approved a Jewish state in Palestine.[20] In 1919 he disparaged Palestinian identity. *Zionism, be it right or wrong, good or bad, is rooted in age-long traditions, in present needs, in future hopes, of far greater import than the desires and prejudices of the 700,000 Arabs who now inhabit that ancient land.* Rashid Khalidi tartly comments: *For Balfour, the Zionists had traditions, needs, and hopes; the Arabs of Palestine (who 'now' – i.e. recently – inhabited the country) only desires and prejudices.*[21]

The Zionist Purchasing Agency would sell only to Jews. Many peasants were evicted, with violent clashes between peasants and Jewish landowners. In 1899 a former mayor of Jerusalem, Yusuf al-Din al Khalidi, warned Herzl of war: *In theory, Zionism is an absolutely natural and just idea on how to solve the Jewish question. Yet it is impossible to overlook the actual reality, which must be taken into account. Palestine is an integral part of the Ottoman Empire and today it is inhabited by non-Jews ... By what right do the Jews want it for themselves? ... The only way to take it is by force, using canons and warships.*[22]

Under Britain's League of Nations Mandate to administer Palestine, it did not help that Britain had promised the land for a Jewish state and for an Arab one. Conflict grew worse. Some 740 were dead after riots in 1929 at the al-Aqsa mosque and the Wailing Wall. A 1937 Royal Commission reported about a million Arabs in conflict with 400,000 Jews. After the Nazi atrocities, many Jewish refugees came to Palestine/Israel. Arab armies invaded. The Israeli 'War of Independence'/the Palestinian 'Nakba' (catastrophe) ended with a decisive Israeli victory. Palestinian loss of far more territory than under the UN plan increased their nationalist backlash.

Raja Shehadeh

The Palestinian sense of homeland includes Jerusalem and other cities and towns. It centres also on the landscape: its beauty and the impress of earlier generations. Raja Shehadeh is a lawyer and a leading writer. His ancestors farmed land around Ramallah. In the nineteenth century they moved to Jaffa. In 1948, his grandfather, a judge, and his father, a lawyer, were forced out of Jaffa. His father returned to Ramallah, where Raja was born. He loved walking in the hills. Sometimes he found round stone buildings like miniature castles where farmers had kept their produce. He knew that Ayoub Ameen, his grandfather's cousin, had made one. With his young wife Zariefeh, Ayoub had built and made its garden. After Ayoub's first night spent there, *when he woke up to a dewy, cool morning he thought he was in Paradise. He loved being out in the hills. His young wife was next to him, they were on their own land.*[23] When the work was finished, he and Zariefeh had celebrated by dancing round their new home until they dropped.

Raja found one of these buildings with the remains of a garden: terraces, flowers, olive trees, ponds and a spring. Indoors he sat on a window-ledge and looked across the valley the owner must have cultivated. It seemed as if *time was petrified into an eternal present, making it possible for me to reconnect with my dead ancestor through this architectural wonder.*[24] He noticed a large soil-covered rock at an odd angle in the garden. Scraping the soil away, he found the rock had been hollowed out to form two arms and a seat. Trying it, he found himself sitting in a very comfortable chair. It gave exactly the support his back needed. Its height was just right for his short legs, and the arms could have been made for him. He knew Ayoub had been a short man and Raja remembered hearing he had made himself a throne to sit on. *As I sat there ... the whispers of the pine trees sounded like the conversation of a family gathered in a circle in their garden.*[25]

The calm of this homeland was threatened. Raja read the plan for settling in the hills 80,000 Jews in twenty-five settlements. He was a lawyer for Palestinians whose land was confiscated. He came to think that judges were unwilling to stand up for Palestinian legal rights against a determined government.

The settlements, outside the boundaries of Israel and illegal under international law, expanded quickly. In 2009, Tony Judt pointed out that for twenty years their population had grown by 5 per cent a year, three times the rate of the general Israeli population. He said the one at Maale Adumim covered more than thirty square miles: *one and a half times the size of Manhattan and nearly half as big as the borough and city of Manchester, England. Some 'settlement'.*[26] But Raja Shehadeh stays loyal to his increasingly submerged homeland, walking there with friends every Friday, not knowing why they still hope for a future there.

Mahmoud Darwish

Mahmoud Darwish was a poet whose power comes over even in translation. Many poems reflect his exile and losing a home. He and his family lived in the village of al-Birwa. He was six when they fled as the Israeli army took it. *No one remembers how we went out the door like a gust of wind.*[27] Some villagers stayed and fought back. The Israelis recaptured the village, with many casualties. As a result, an Israeli soldier later told Darwish: *We blew it up. Raked the stones out of its earth, then ploughed it until it disappeared under the trees.*[28]

At school he stood out, begging for food and clothes. He had left things in the village. Perhaps by going back to fetch them he would show he was not different from the others. In 1949 he and his family did go back. But, having missed Israel's first Arab census, they were refused Israeli nationality. Regulations forbade return to their village, so they were there illegally. They lived as refugees in their own country. At his elementary school, on a day celebrating the founding of Israel, Darwish recited his first poem. It included:

> *You have a house and I have none.*
> *You have celebrations but I have none.*
> *Why can't we play together?*

The response was not good. *I said some words against the government and its victory, and against oppression and colonization.* The military governor sent for him, rebuked and struck him, saying he would stop his father working in the quarry. *At home my father was supportive and said 'God will provide'.*[29]

Several times Darwish was imprisoned for leaving Haifa without a permit. Communist Party members included Arabs and Jews. He joined and edited their newspaper. Refused university in Israel, he studied political economy in Moscow. But he found Moscow was not heaven and left for Cairo. He was denied entry to Israel for twenty-six years after joining the Palestine Liberation Organization. On its executive committee, he wrote the 1988 Algiers Declaration proclaiming Palestinian statehood. An attached document accepts co-existence with Israel in its pre-1967 borders. (Darwish's attitudes suggest he was behind the thinking. About suicide bombing he wrote: *We have to understand – not justify – what gives rise to this tragedy.* After 9/11 he wrote in a Palestinian newspaper that nothing justifies terrorism.) For the Declaration's conciliatory parts, one day he should be honoured by Palestinians and Israelis at peace with each other.

Darwish felt constrained as the semi-official poet of the Palestinian cause. He felt poetry, through local experience, should touch the universal. With a poet deeply in his own culture, you shouldn't stumble over the differences: *the particular and deep experiencer of this poet gives you the opportunity to encounter an entire universal culture ... I aspire to root my truth in the human and the universal and not in some fixed and limited interpretation.*[30]

In 1966 he was allowed back to visit his family. Thousands of Palestinians cheered him and chanted his poems. Afterwards he said: *As long as my soul is alive no-one can smother my feeling for my country which I still consider as Palestine.* Huge audiences at many meetings heard him speak for them. But the spokesman was always rooted in his own experience of loss and exile:

> *I belong there. I have many memories. I was born as*
>   *everyone was born.*
> *I have a mother, a house with many windows, brothers,*
>   *friends, and a prison cell*
> *With a chilly window! ...*
> *I have lived on the land long before swords turned man into*
>   *prey.*
> *I belong there ...*
> *To break the rules, I have learned all the words needed for a*
>   *trial by blood.*
> *I have learned and dismantled all the words in order to*
>   *draw from them a single word: Home.*[31]

2
WOUNDS AND BACKLASH

I: Cycles of Violence: The Classic Pattern: Germany and France, 1807–1945

Between national groups, what is a cycle of violence? It often starts with wounds. The backlash starts the next round of conflict. Defeat's bitterness outlasts victory's exhilaration. In 1989, Slobodan Milosevic, stirring Serbian nationalism, made an emotionally charged speech at a huge rally on the anniversary of the Serbian defeat on the Field of the Blackbirds by the Turks *in 1389, six hundred years earlier.* Each cycle has its own features. The common pattern is probably as old as human history.

1807: French-Occupied Berlin: 'Unmake What Has Happened'

The early philosopher of German nationalism was Johann Gottlieb Fichte. *Addresses to the German Nation* grew from his 1807 lectures in Berlin occupied by Napoleon's army. He urged action ... *to unmake what has happened, eradicating this dishonourable interlude from the annals of the Germans.*[1]

1870–71: The Franco–Prussian War

The Franco–Prussian War was an early start on modern national warfare, in which Germany's victory has been seen as a disaster: for herself and the entire world.[2]

The French army moved first. But Bismarck had used a dispute over a Hohenzollern becoming King of Spain to provoke war. He made public a humiliating telegram dismissing the French ambassador, rightly telling his friends this would be a red rag to the Gallic bull.[3]

Towards The Dark Centre of The Cycle: 'Defensive' Strangulation

The dark centre of the cycle starts as attitudes and intentions. The Prussians feared a warlike France. The war minister said the only peace they could conclude must dismember France. Another leader said they should *treat the French as a conquered army and demoralize them to the utmost of our ability. We ought to crush them so that they will not be able to breathe for a hundred years.*[4] When Prussia started war successfully, parallel French sentiments were expressed. Leon Gambetta said: *Since the war has become a war of extermination covertly prepared by Prussia for thirty years past, we must for the security of our people and for the honour of France, finish for good with this odious people.*[5]

Given opportunity, dark attitudes start to shape policy. After the 1871 French defeat, a third of France was occupied. The Prussian army (eradicating memory of Berlin's occupation?) had a victory march down the Champs-Élysées. France had to pay reparations and to give much of Alsace and Lorraine to Germany. The Chief of the German General staff, Moltke, was harsh towards unofficial resisters, proposing to destroy the buildings they used or even the whole village. He predicted shooting every inhabitant. From Berlin headquarters General Sheridan supported *causing the inhabitants so much suffering that they must long for peace … The people must be left with nothing but their eyes to weep with over the war.*[6]

'You Cannot See Beyond the End of Your Noses'

One German who saw further than those who celebrated victory was Friedrich Engels. From London he wrote to his brother Rudolf in Germany: *The fact is that you cannot see beyond the end of your noses. You have made sure that for many years to come France (which after all lies on your border) will remain your enemy.*[7] Bismarck was among many not seeing beyond the end of their noses. French resentment and fear of repetition (and perhaps too the hope of regaining Alsace and Lorraine) led to alliances with Russia, Britain and others. Germany saw this as 'encirclement', which contributed to war in 1914.

1918: The Railway Coach and the Fallen Eagle

When World War I ended, Germans surrendered to Marshal Foch and allies in a railway coach at Compiègne. This time could the French leaders see beyond the end of their noses? At the Versailles Conference, the French wanted Germany punished. They obstructed food supplies to relieve hunger perhaps caused by the continuing British naval blockade.[8] The site of the surrender was a place of French celebration and German humiliation. The proud German eagle was laid low.

Harold Nicholson, a British delegate at Versailles, saw President Woodrow Wilson's mind as blurred by religion. *He was able, as are all very religious men, to attribute unto God the things that are Caesar's: he was able to convince himself, in ardent agonies of soul, that his own principles had not been violated.*[9] Maynard Keynes too saw Wilson's mind as *essentially theological not intellectual with all the strengths and weaknesses of that manner of thought* and so always outwitted by France's Prime Minister, Clemenceau. Keynes gave a vivid portrait of Clemenceau believing *the German understands and can understand nothing but intimidation, that he is without generosity or remorse in negotiation, that there is no advantage he will not take of you, and no extent to which he will not demean himself for profit, that he is without honour, pride or mercy. Therefore you must never negotiate with a German or conciliate him; you must dictate to him.* Destroying the German economy would defend France.

Figure 2: The Alsace-Lorraine Monument
© Fab5669 via Wikimedia Commons (Attribution-ShareAlike 4.0
International license: https://commons.wikimedia.org/wiki/File:Compi
%C3%A8gne_-_clairi%C3%A8re_de_l%27Armistice_18.jpg)

*He sees the issue in terms of France and Germany, not of
humanity or of European civilization ... The war has bitten
into his consciousness somewhat differently from ours.*[10]

The emphasis on Clemenceau's cynical ruthlessness may
under-rate the cycle of violence in his reaction to Germany.
Margaret Macmillan points out how much more France had
suffered from the war than the other allies.[11] France lost the
highest percentage of population: a quarter of Frenchmen
between eighteen and thirty. Six thousand square miles of
France (previously producing 20 per cent of its crops) were
ruined. And much more. None of the delegates will have
thought in terms of humiliation and backlash. But it is hard
not to see the cycle in Clemenceau.

The outcome for Germany was harsh. As well as losing Alsace and Lorraine, Germany had to pay enormous reparations and sign the 'war guilt' clauses: a humiliating acceptance that the war was all Germany's fault.

1940: *The Tablet on the Ground*

The German backlash was strong. In *Mein Kampf* Hitler raged at the humiliations. Undoing them was his life project, one with huge appeal in Germany. Leni Riefenstahl's brilliant but evil film of a Nuremberg rally, *Triumph of the Will*, presented the humiliations of 1918 as being expunged by Nazi-led renewal.

After the 1940 French defeat, Hitler created for them an operatic humiliation. They signed the armistice in the Compiègne railway carriage, with Hitler in Marshall Foch's seat. As Hitler arrived, the fallen German eagle was hidden by the swastika.

Im Walde von Compiègne wurde am 21. Juni 1940 durch den Führer des Großdeutschen Reiches Adolf Hitler die Schmach von 1918 ausgelöscht

Figure 3: Postcard showing monument draped in a swastika flag

What was not hidden was the triumphalist monument on the ground. It read: ICI LE 11 NOVEMBRE 1918 SUCCOMBA LE CRIMINAL ORGEUIL DE L'EMPIRE ALLEMAND VAINCU PAR LES PEUPLES LIBRES OU IL PRETENDAIT ASSERVIR. (Here on 11 November 1918 succumbed the criminal vanity of the German Empire, defeated by the free peoples that it claimed to enslave.)

William Shirer, CBS radio correspondent, described Hitler's face. *It was grave, solemn, yet brimming with revenge* ... Hitler stood on the 1918 monument on the ground. Shirer said: *I have seen that face many times at the great moments of his life. But today! It is afire with scorn, anger, hate, revenge, triumph. He steps off the monument and contrives to make even this gesture a masterpiece of contempt. He glances back at it, contemptuous, angry, – angry, you almost feel, because he cannot wipe out the awful, provoking lettering with one sweep of his high Prussian boot.*[12]

1962: Escape: Two Tablets on the Ground at Reims Cathedral

Not all cycles have such an end. The French–German cycle lasted nearly a century and a half. It took a world war, in which the two countries in turn experienced devastating defeats, before both sides saw ending the cycle as an overriding imperative. For Israel and Palestine, the hope must be for both nations to see the cycle for what it is without having to go through such catastrophes.

Figure 4: Memorial tablets at Reims Cathedral
(Photographs by author.)

II: Where the Cycle Sometimes Takes Palestinians and Israelis

Jonathan Freedland described photographs of four teenage boys: *They are brimming with life. Except these four boys are dead. Naftali Frankel, Gilad Shaar, and Eyal Yifrach were murdered first, their bodies found on Monday, and Mohamed Abu Khdeir was murdered after that, his life apparently taken in revenge for the other three … their lives were ended by people capable of believing that to slaughter an innocent child is a noble act of service, somehow a good deed in the cause of the nation.*[13]

Where the Cycle Takes Some Israelis: The Occupied Territories on the West Bank

In 2005, Palestinians at Mufaqara saw an Israeli settler walking carefully through their fields. Afterwards their sheep fell sick and some died. Large amounts of barley had been soaked in rat poison and spread on the fields. The aim was to force Palestinians off the land by killing their sheep and goats. Later some shepherds took their flocks to a (once Palestinian) field, but the settlers pelted them with stones. One shepherd raged: *Why do they attack us wherever we go? I am tired of this, day after day, tired of being stoned and poisoned and shot at.*[14] Visiting Ramallah, with the help of my Israeli hosts, I was shown by one of my Palestinian hosts a settlement on top of a hill. He indicated a point beyond which Palestinians would risk being shot.

Not all the mistreatment of Palestinians comes from 'unofficial' acts of settler hostility. In November 2020, Yvonne Helle, the UN humanitarian coordinator for the occupied Palestinian territory, reported that Israeli forces demolished a Palestinian village. They left 32 adults and 41 children homeless. After the demolition, families, including children, were seem examining their wrecked possessions in the wind as the rain started. The villagers' livelihood comes from sheep. Israel has declared that part of the Jordan valley a firing zone for army training. Official policy is that buildings there without permission may be demolished. Yvonne Helle said *Palestinians can almost never obtain such permits*, and up to that point in 2020 demolitions had left 869 Palestinians homeless: *Demolitions are a key means of creating an environment designed to coerce Palestinians to leave their homes.* The Israeli human rights organization B'Tselem said the demolition included 18 tents and sheds lived in by 11 families, as well as a shed for livestock and storage. They destroyed food for livestock and confiscated a vehicle and two tractors. A spokesperson for B'Tselem said that *as part of its efforts to take over more and more Palestinian land, Israel routinely demolishes Palestinian homes and property.*[15]

The Protection of Civilians: The Fourth Geneva Convention

The occupying power shall not deport or transfer parts of its own civilian population into the territory it occupies.

The territories were occupied as a result of the 1967 Six-Day War. The start of that war was disputed. There was an Israeli strike on Egyptian planes on military airfields. Egypt called this unjustified. Israel called it pre-emptive defence against attack. Israel's narrative had some decent support. There were good reasons for expecting Egypt might start a war. President Nasser of Egypt said he was willing to fight Israel. Egypt had expelled UN peacekeepers from Sinai and blockaded Israel's route to the Red Sea.

From the claim the war was defensive, some Israelis have drawn conclusions about the territories Israel then occupied. Dore Gold, President of the Jerusalem Center for Public Affairs, said that, after a defensive war, they should be called not 'occupied territories' but 'disputed territories'. *By repeatedly pointing to 'occupation' they manage to reverse the causality of the conflict … Thus the current territorial dispute is allegedly the result of an Israeli decision to 'occupy' rather than the result of a war imposed on Israel by a coalition of Arab states in 1967.*[16] If others started the war, does this really show Israel does not occupy the territories? Was Germany not occupied by the Allies after 1945?

'Disputed territories' would let Israeli governments say the Geneva Convention does not apply. Israeli settlements in occupied territories flout the Convention. Dore Gold's weak reason for rejecting it does not change this. And a coldly legalistic approach excludes human realities. Why not mention that rescuing mutually entrapped peoples needs solutions giving enough land to each? In arguing against a *legal* requirement to respect the Convention, it would not come amiss to say that, as a people who have not lost their humanity, *of course* Israel should respect it.

Where The Cycle Takes Some Palestinians

Kanan Makiya was concerned about his own side: how Palestinian nationalism was developing. It *was forged and hammered into the prickly and defensive thing that we see today in the crucible of its denial by Zionism. The more it was attacked, the more powerful and politically regressive it grew. These are perfectly natural, all-too-human responses to denial of identity through aggression ... they are also breeding grounds for nationalist, religious, and ethnic fanaticism.*[17]

The urge to revenge deaths and humiliations may become more lethal through underlying despair. One response is denial. Palestine shares this with some other Arab countries. It is seen in reluctance even to name Israel, calling it only 'the Zionist entity'. A friend of mine, critical of Israel, gave a lecture in Beirut. He was shouted down by demonstrators. Scouring the many items in his CV, they found he had advised the Hebrew University of Jerusalem on some matter. As a result, despite his considerable sympathy for the Palestinian cause, they would not accept his invitation to dialogue. After shouting him down they left. He also learnt that in Lebanon it is *illegal* to have any contact at all with Israel.[18] Another response is rage and cruelty towards Palestinians 'collaborating' with Israelis. In the First Intifada, a pregnant mother of four was found hanged from a tree for this. Kanan Makiya says investigation by the Palestinian journalist Bassam Eid showed the mother was not a collaborator. (But even if she had been ...?)

Antisemitism

The cycle leads some Palestinians into dark places, including antisemitism. This affects Hamas, but even leaders of Fatah can succumb to it. In 1983, Mahmoud Abbas wrote a preface to a pamphlet on the gas chambers by the holocaust denier Robert Faurisson.[19] In 1984 he published his doctoral dissertation suggesting the holocaust was supported by a tacit alliance of Nazis and Zionists. He later expressed regret about the book.[20] But in 2018, as President of Palestine, he said in a speech: *From the eleventh century until the holocaust that took place in Germany, those Jews – who moved to western and eastern Europe – were subjected to a massacre every ten to fifteen years. But why did this happen? They say, 'It is because we are Jews'.* He suggested that *hostility to Jews is not because of their religion, but rather their social function*, which he described as *usury and banking and such*.[21] He later apologized. But, apology or not, there seems something dark about a mental climate where someone thought fit to be President could make these comments. Other antisemitism can be cruder and without apology. In Jiljilya in the West Bank a poster was written in English: *I love to kill Jews.*[22]

Nonie Darwish's father, very senior in Egyptian military intelligence, started the Fedayeen movement that made attacks into Israel. He was killed when Nonie was eight. She remembered President Nasser and various high officials coming to the house and asking: *Which one of you will avenge your father's death by killing Jews?* She describes her schooling. Jews were evil and God's enemies. Making peace with them would be weakness, and not to hate them a sin. They were unclean. Touch them and you should wash. Lessons, songs and films were about jihad and destroying Israel. *We recited jihadist poetry every day, and some of the girls cried when we had to pledge jihad to give up our life to be a martyr.* Loudspeakers blared *May Allah destroy the infidels and the Jews, the enemies of Allah. We are not to befriend them or to make treaties with them.*[23]

Nonie Darwish remembered how Israeli commandos, responding to an attack, came to their house. Her father was away. *They left us – the women and children – unharmed. I was grateful that the Israeli soldiers did not kill us, especially because the Fedayeen had killed so many Israeli civilians, including women and children ... Israel is not perfect. But when my brother collapsed and was given a three per cent chance to live, he was taken to Hadassah University*

*Hospital, and the Jewish doctors saved his life; they treated
the son of a jihad. In that time of health crisis, an Arab could
trust Jews.*[24]

*Where the Cycle Took Both Sides at Jenin Refugee Camp:
The 2002 Assault and After*

After a deadly terrorist attack, the Israeli Defence Force,
or IDF, reoccupied the West Bank in 'Operation Defensive
Shield'. They assaulted the refugee camp at Jenin, the source
of many terrorist attacks. Their claim about this was endorsed
by Human Rights Watch: *Palestinian gunmen did endanger
Palestinian civilians in the camp by using it as a base for
planning and launching attacks.*[25] Kamal Anis testified that
he *saw the Israeli soldiers pile 30 bodies beneath a half-
wrecked house. When the pile was complete, they bulldozed
the building, bringing its ruins down on the corpses. Then
they flattened the area with a tank.* A Palestinian official
said 500 Palestinians were killed. Another put the figure at
thousands.[26]

David Holley, a British army major and adviser to
Amnesty, visited Jenin. Clearly civilians were killed. *The
bodies are there to be seen. You have children, women, old
men and cripples, so clearly these were not fighters.* But he
thought that, in intensive fighting, they could have been
killed in crossfire: *talking to witnesses ... it just appears
there was no wholesale killing.*[27] A report by Human
Rights Watch said there was no massacre.[28] So did the UN,
suggesting 52 Palestinians (mainly armed) were killed, as
were 23 IDF soldiers. Sharon Sadeh, London correspondent
of the liberal Israeli paper *Ha'aretz*, strongly criticized some
British papers (*The Times, Independent* and *Guardian*) who
had accepted this 'massacre'. He said they were *quick to
demonize Israel* with *sensational accusations based on thin
evidence.*[29]

David Holley and Human Rights Watch, while rejecting
the 'massacre', did not exonerate the IDF from war crimes.
David Holley said that *Water and electricity were cut off to
the town ... That cannot be denied and that is a war crime
... for nine days no wounded were taken to the hospital, the
Israelis blocked it. That is a fact. That is a war crime.* Human

Rights Watch said many civilian deaths were unlawful killings by the IDF. Kamal Zgheir *was shot and run over by a tank on a major road outside the camp ... even though he had a white flag attached to his wheelchair.* Jamal Fayid, a paralysed man, was *crushed in the rubble of his home ... despite his family's pleas to be allowed to remove him.* They mentioned many credible reports of the IDF using Palestinians as human shields. Kamal Tawalbi described being put on the balcony with his back to the street, the soldier using his shoulder to rest his rifle as he fired. His fourteen-year-old son *was in the same position ... the soldier had his gun on his shoulder and he was shooting.*[30]

After Jenin

Terrorist attacks from Jenin triggered the IDF assault. Later, Tuha Aziz said why she became a suicide bomber: *My reasons are obvious: the massacre in Jenin, in Jabilya, in Nablus, Gaza and Ramallah. There is no hope for peace because the Jews have no heart ... every Palestinian knows there is no chance to make peace with them.*[31] The hostile stereotypes are alive. Giving reasons, the first name Tuha Aziz cited was Jenin. The cycle rolled on.

III: Mindsets and the Media

Some people are shaped in ways that, without the cycle, they might not have wished: One woman ('a very generous, loving and kind person who has worked with Israelis for years'): *I know it is not a good thing to feel this way, but it's human. I can't help myself either. When I hear of it, I think, 'Is there no better way?' But when I see the images on television I feel, 'Good for them! Let them feel pain too.'*[32]

Printing presses helped Europeans create their nations. The greater power of television can be misused to bias how people see their imagined community. Study of this has been greatly influenced by the 'propaganda model' of Edward S. Herman and Noam Chomsky.[33] They see the main bias as propaganda for the interests of those with wealth and power. There is truth in this but it is not the whole story.

The Israeli former news editor Daniel Dor mentions a more subtle bias.[34] Journalists often need to please corporations or owners, but they also need to please audiences or readers. People's identity is linked to their national community. They need to know how the nation as a whole answers certain questions. What unites their society or tears it apart? Who do they trust? What do they fear? What will they talk about? What would they prefer not to hear? Dor says: *More than anything else, the perspectives offered by the different media are assertions about what it should feel like to be Israeli.*[35] People turn to the media for answers. Dor thinks the media tacitly *guarantee to answer them in the way they are most likely to be answered by other members of the group.* The guarantee is not explicit. But media power comes from people's need to know their nation's mindset. The price journalism pays for this is keeping close to their society's conventional views, in Israel including Palestinian issues. I know nothing about the Palestinian media, but would be surprised if they were exempt from criticisms parallel to Dor's of Israeli media.

Dor said Israeli reporting of Jenin reflected and sustained a siege mentality. He saw suppression of guilt about treatment of Palestinians. Perhaps the most extreme was the paper *Ma'ariv*. (I cannot speak or understand Hebrew, and was not in Jenin or in Israel/Palestine in 2002. I have assumed that Dor gives an accurate account of these media reports and opinions. Readers without these limitations may want to check for themselves, comparing Dor's book with their own experience of the Israeli media or by looking at reviews.[36]) *Ma'ariv*'s editor-in-chief, Amnon Danker, wrote that *this is a Zionist supplement, if you pardon the term, patriotic – God forbid.* Why the false apology? He expected his readers to accept the Zionism and patriotism. He was inviting readers to endorse the decision to offend un-named *others* who would disagree. It was a gesture to an assumed 'we', proud to defy a hostile world.

Guilt can be dispelled in some by reassurance that most of the nation, especially soldiers, are behind the policy. Prime Minister Sharon's visit to reservist troops was reported under the headline 'A Warm Welcome'. The soldiers have no doubts: *We didn't ask why, we just came.* A colonel is quoted: *I have no moral qualms. I have only one moral obligation – towards my kids and my home. My only commitment in this war is to them.* Troops are quoted as telling Sharon: *Conscientious objection is a marginal phenomenon. We, here, are giving the answer on the ground, by our very numbers.* Reporters were barred from the combat zone. Stories came from the IDF.

Dor said that half the headlines in *Ma'ariv* mentioning Palestinians are about generous acts by soldiers or Israeli civilians: *Terror victim's family will meet Arab woman who received his kidney donation; Soldiers evacuated house in Bethlehem – gave family 1500 shekels; Army doctor delivered baby of Jerusalem suicide bomber's relative.* The stories may well be true. But should *half* the Palestinian-related headlines be like this? Dor quotes Aviv Lavie in *Ha'aretz* saying that, on TV stations round the world, *we could see IDF soldiers taking over hospitals, damaging medical equipment and medicine, locking up doctors and keeping them away from their patients … the entire world sees injured Palestinians bleeding on the streets, and hears accounts about the IDF stopping ambulances on their way to treat them.*

Mindsets Challenged: 'Breaking the Silence'

Palestinians have long protested against their treatment by the IDF. Some soldiers too have protested. Most Israeli citizens of the right age are conscripted. The soldiers are close to a cross-section of young Israelis. Some (not all) have been appalled by things they have been required to do. In 2004, sixty IDF veterans who had served in Hebron in the occupied West Bank founded *Breaking the Silence*. They publish verbatim testimonies of participants and eye-witnesses to encourage debate about the occupiers' methods.

Some testimonies are in their book *Our Harsh Logic:*[37] *There was a lot of joy at people's misery, guys were happy talking about it. There was a moment where someone they knew was mentally ill yelled at the soldiers, but one soldier decided that he was going to beat him up anyway, so they smashed him. They hit him in the head with the butt of a*

gun, he was bleeding ... There were a pile of arrest orders signed by the battalion commander, ready ... They'd fill in that the person was detained on suspicion of disturbing the peace.[38]
Some people are like ... 'Okay, I killed a kid, okay'. They laugh. Some people take it hard ... They also say that if anyone jumps on the APC and takes the machine guns ... shoot to kill ... a friend of mine came with his M24 ... and just then a kid climbed up. He shot him, all happy – 'I took someone down'. And then they told him he took down an eleven-year-old kid ... He took it very hard.[39]

All this may stimulate the cycle of violence, to which some soldiers, because of their humanity, contribute less or not at all. Among the testimonies in *Our Harsh Logic* are those from soldiers not cold to how victims feel, or to how victims saw them. One reported the treatment of people arriving in Palestinian ambulances at checkpoints they were not allowed to pass: *The patient had to walk some twenty meters to the other ambulance or be carried on a gurney. Now, I don't know if you've ever seen a ninety-year-old woman cross a checkpoint with an IV in her arm, but it's not a pretty sight. And the accusing look in the eye of a ninety-year-old woman is something that stays with you.*[40]

Some were aware of the responses when the soldiers destroyed a house. *They smash the floors, turn over sofas, throw plants and pictures, turn over beds, smash the closets, the tiles. There were other, smaller things, but this really bothered me. The look on the people whose house you've gone into. It really hurt me to see this. And after all that, they left them for hours, tied up and blindfolded in the school ... The way they looked at us, what was going through their minds, their children's minds.*[41]

IV: Eyeless in Gaza

Pretend it is obvious that the Biblical Israelites and Philistines were ancestors of the Israelis and Palestinians. Compared to now, power then was reversed. The Israelite hero Samson was captured and blinded by the Philistines. With Samson their prisoner, they *when their hearts were merry ... said, Call*

*for Samson, that he may make us sport ... and they set him
between the pillars.* And Samson called on God: *I pray thee,
only this once, O God, that I may be at once avenged of the
Philistines for my two eyes. And Samson took hold of the two
middle pillars upon which the house stood ... And Samson
said, Let me die with the Philistines. And he bowed himself
with all his might; and the house fell upon the lords, and upon
all the people that were therein. So the dead which he slew
at his death were more than they which he slew in his life.*[42]
John Milton put into Samson's mouth these words:

*... Promise was that I
Should Israel from Philistian yoke deliver!
Ask for this great Deliverer now, and find him
Eyeless, in Gaza, at the mill, with slaves,
Himself in bonds under Philistian yoke*

And added, *But what is strength without a double dose of
wisdom?*[43]
In the days of the story, both sides had little wisdom.
Reading the Book of Judges, or John Milton, the thought
may come that now in Gaza many on both sides also seem
blind.

Hamas and Antisemitism

Hamas runs Gaza. Their Constitution says of Jews: *Only
when they have completely digested the area on which
they will have laid their hand, they will look forward to
more expansion, etc. Their scheme has been laid out in The
Protocols of the Elders of Zion, and their present [conduct]
is the best proof of what is said there* (Hamas Constitution,
Article 32). The *Protocols* were an early twentieth-century
fraudulent account of Jews conspiring to rule the world. For
Hitler, they showed that *the whole existence of this people
is based on a continuous lie.* Revealing one attitude to
evidence, he thought claims they were forged were *the best
proof that they are authentic.*[44] In May 1943, the machinery
of the Holocaust was being powered up to enable even
more killing. At Auschwitz, they were adding three new
gas chambers, making nine furnaces in total.[45] That month,

Goebbels gave a glimpse of the thinking behind the killing: *The Protocols of Zion are as modern today as they were when published ... At noon I mentioned this to the Fuehrer. He believes the Protocols are absolutely genuine ... In all the world, he said, the Jews are alike, etc., etc. ... There is therefore no other recourse for modern nations than to exterminate the Jew.*[46]

The Hamas Constitution was agreed in 1988. Did they really not know the document's dark history? By now they will have heard. Challenged, one former Hamas leader, Dr Razeq, asked for patience, saying Hamas had been *looking into changing or modifying this charter.* He added: *We need time to adjust.*[47] Have the years since 1988 really not left a few spare days – or a few spare minutes – to remove article 32?

Israel and Gaza: Occupation, Withdrawal, Blockade

Israeli occupation was a disaster for Palestinians in Gaza. Among many Israeli forms of domination, house searches were just one. Amira Hass, reporter for the Israeli paper *Ha'aretz* in Gaza, saw three different Palestinian homes just after being searched by Israeli soldiers for wanted men. She said these searches were typical of hundreds. *A large group of soldiers ... would break into the house, usually in the middle of the night ... and let loose an orgy of shouting and destruction, emptying wardrobes and tearing them apart (conceivably weapons might be hidden inside), spraying the thin walls and ceilings with gunfire (there could be a double ceiling),* But these conceivable justifications could hardly apply to the totally destroyed televisions, radios and furniture, to the shattered mirrors or to the phone cables ripped from the walls.[48]

In 2003, Hamas declared a unilateral ceasefire. Later, Israel, under Ariel Sharon's government, withdrew both army and settlers from the Gaza Strip, leaving Palestinians in control – with the important exceptions of borders, airspace and territorial waters. Withdrawal had many opponents in Israel. The government's case was that, if the two peoples occupied the same territory, Palestinians would campaign for one man one vote: That *would signal the end of the Jewish state for us.* A separation *would surely prevent a conversation with the Palestinians for at least 25 years.*[49]

Others claimed withdrawal would prevent any Palestinian state. Dov Weisglass, adviser to the Prime Minister, said: *The significance of the disengagement plan is that it will halt the peace process ... In effect, the entire package known as the Palestinian state, with all that it involves, has been removed from our agenda indefinitely ... The formation of a Palestinian state, with all the security threats that involves, is the goal of the peace process ... all of that has now been blocked.*[50]

What was not halted was the violence. In 2008, Hamas rocket attacks ended a six-month ceasefire, causing terror in Sderot and other border towns. Israel hit back with Operation Cast Lead: *air strikes the length and breadth of the Gaza Strip which destroyed or damaged nearly every Palestinian security installation.*[51] Avi Shlaim has said the operation was not war but massacre, *pounding the densely populated strip from the air, sea and land for 22 days.* He gives the numbers killed. Israelis 13. Palestinians: 1,417 including 313 children.[52]

Israel started its blockade of Gaza in 2007, eighteen months before Operation Cast Lead. The case for it was to exclude weapons being sent to Gaza by sea. Lawyers disagreed over whether Israel had the right to do that. But the scope of the blockade raised doubts about whether weapons were its sole target. In 2010, six ships bound for Gaza with ten thousand tons of food and other non-military supplies were attacked by Israeli forces, killing nine people on the leading ship, the Mavi Marmara.[53]

Was part of the intention not to block only weapons but also to deprive Palestinians of essentials? Sara Roy introduced the concept of 'de-development', which she defines as *the deliberate, systematic and progressive dismemberment of an indigenous economy by a dominant one, where economic – and by extension, societal – potential is not only distorted but denied.* She claims that this is one of Israel's policies: *they have taken from the indigenous population its most critical economic resources, namely land, water and labor, and the capacity and potential for developing those resources. ... De-development ensures that there will be no economic base*

– even one that is malformed – to support an independent indigenous economy (and society).[54]

My first reaction was sceptical. There are many Israelis who would be appalled by such a policy. But government policies do not always reflect the views of decent people, however many. And some evidence supports Sara Roy's suggestion. There is the affair of the Mavi Marmara. There is the lack of concern about Palestinian drinking water. In 1996, Amira Hass described it. *The tap water in most Gazan homes is salty and the bad taste is more noticeable in tea. Even the 'sweet' water is contaminated with sewage – causing, at the very least, intestinal trouble. Anyone who can afford a substitute finds one.*[55]

Dov Weisglass made a cold joke: one disguising cruelty as humour. The disguise is not serious: the victim is not meant to smile or laugh, but to feel humiliated. It is one way the stronger can dominate the weaker. Israel's blockade limits the food in Gaza. In 2016 Weisglass, adviser to Prime Ministers, was widely quoted saying the policy aimed to 'put the Palestinians on a diet but not to make them die of hunger'. The 'joke' taunts opponents with our power over what you eat, and our amusing thought of calling it 'putting you on a diet'.

The 2021 Israel–Hamas War

Not all Israelis near Gaza feel the tough responses make them more secure. One, Nomika Zion, wrote this nine years before the 2021 war: *Never have I felt an ounce of security when our planes passed over the skies of Sderot at night en route to Gaza to 'crush the head of the snake' ... I didn't feel safer when two hundred homes were flattened on a cold winter night in 2004, leaving two thousand refugees without shelter; when the Gaza power station was bombed, leaving half a million people without electricity. I gained no sense of tranquillity when the bulldozers razed homes, sweeping up fields, orchards and chicken coops; when tanks fired without pause.*[56]

There were two immediate causes of the 2021 conflict. An anticipated Israeli Supreme Court decision could lead to evictions of Palestinian families from their homes in the

Sheikh Jarrah district of East Jerusalem. At protest demonstrations, Palestinians at the Al-Aqsa Mosque threw stones at Israeli police. The police responded (outside and inside the Mosque) with tear gas, stun grenades and rubber bullets. Over 600 people, mainly Palestinians, were injured. Three days later, 300 Palestinians and twenty-one Israeli police were injured.

Violence spread. Israel ignored a Hamas ultimatum to withdraw security forces from Sheikh Jarrah and Temple Mount. Hamas launched rockets against Israel. Some were foiled by Israel's Iron Dome defence system. Others got through, hitting houses and a school. Human Rights Watch saw Hamas's launching of over 4,000 rockets and mortars at population centres in Israel as a war crime, violating the prohibition against deliberate or indiscriminate attacks against civilians.

Israel responded with aerial bombardment of public buildings in Gaza. These included Hamas's headquarters and network of military tunnels, but also six hospitals and Gaza's only COVID clinic. They also hit a building occupied by Al-Jazeera and Associated Press journalists. Human Rights Watch noted an airstrike, apparently using precision-guided bombs, on Al-Wahda street in central Gaza City. They found no evidence of military targets and said no advance evacuation warning was given. Forty-four civilians were killed, including women and children. As with the Hamas bombardment of Israel, there was a potential war crime to investigate: an attack not directed at a specific military objective is unlawful. A ceasefire was agreed.

Both sides claimed victory. The claims were illusory. Israeli bombardment was a disaster for many Palestinians. Family members were lost, as were homes, hospitals and their COVID clinic. The Israeli 'victory' was also a disaster. The degree of penetration of the Iron Dome was unprecedented. For the first time many Palestinian citizens of Israel publicly supported Hamas, raising questions about Israel's future as an internally peaceful state. The episode was ruinous for each side.

The dialogue of the deaf continued. Each cited key events when 'our' side was 'forced' to respond to something terrible by the other side. At the Al-Aqsa Mosque, did police weapons start the violence, or was it started by Palestinians throwing stones? The answer may not be clear, but suppose the stone-throwing came first. It could still be seen as a response to an earlier event. A Ramadan call to worship had been silenced by Israelis cutting the speaker cable so that a speech by Israel's President could be heard without distraction. But perhaps cutting the cable was caused by evidence of Palestinian intention to disrupt the speech. These guesses may all be wrong. But often the question 'who started it?' has no clear answer.

Behind visible causes are background influences. Was the ferocity of Netanyahu's response to Hamas's missiles influenced by a possible boost to his election chances? Did it make a difference that part of Ramadan coincided with a Jerusalem Day march celebrating Israel's capture of East Jerusalem? Often there is a seemingly endless chain of disputes about the past. Who owns the Sheikh Jarrah houses where the Palestinians lived? Arguments sometimes go back to rival Ottoman Empire documents. Easing the grip of all this is easier said than done. It is the elusive process of becoming good neighbours, people who prefer the roughly reasonable compromise to the bitterly precise lawsuit. Or, in this case, prefer it to killing men, women and children on the other side.

V: The Cycle's Dark Centre: Terrorism, Assassination, Torture

It is hard to discuss the dark centre without alienating some on each side. This section of the chapter does not intend to give readers a bad time, but is written partly to challenge a too relaxed view of the cycle's human costs. This is linked to a deeply defended comfort zone that George Orwell saw: *I have little direct evidence about the atrocities in the Spanish Civil War ... But what impressed me then, and has impressed me ever since, is that atrocities are believed in or disbelieved in solely on grounds of political predilection. Everyone believes in the atrocities of the enemy and disbelieves in those of his own side, without ever bothering to examine the evidence.*[57]

Suicide Bombings

Why do some Palestinians become suicide bombers? One soldier questioned for the book *Our Harsh Logic* was asked:
You spat on Jews?
No, why? They didn't do anything to me.
What about the Arabs?
But they're like, Arabs ... the guy I spat on didn't do anything to me. I think he didn't do anything at all. But again, it was cool, and it was the one thing I could do to, you know, I can't go and arrest people and be proud that I caught a terrorist ... But I can spit on them and humiliate them and ridicule them.[58]

Doctor Eyad Sarraj is a Palestinian psychiatrist who treats children for shock. He believed one contribution to their becoming suicide bombers was their fathers' humiliation. Palestinians had become Israeli's slaves, building their houses and sweeping their streets. *No you will never know how painful it is unless your country is occupied by another force. Only then will you learn how to watch in silence pretending not to see the torture of your friends and the humiliation of your father. Do you know what it means for a child to see his father spat at and beaten by an Israeli soldier?* For Palestinian children the intifada only resulted in them throwing stones and being killed.

After Oslo, Palestinians were buoyed by the hope of peace: *no more curfews and we could actually spend our evening or wander in streets which were now ours after eight o'clock at night ...* But *Binyamin Netanyahu refused to free our prisoners ... He even surrounded our towns and villages with his tanks and arrested our policemen ... we were humiliated, even arrested and tortured by Palestinian forces to protect the peace. Our Authority was turning against us to please Netanyahu. Our officials were driving in big cars and building big villas. They have VIP cards and cross the check posts like human beings while we are left to rot ... Now do you understand why we have turned into suicide killers?*[59]

When the 2000 Intifada started, Roney Srour, a Palestinian psychotherapist, felt torn. His own people were traumatized by fifty years of conflict and the destruction of so much of their society. Occupation made them unsafe. Coping with the death of people close while struggling to support their families often left them helpless, depressed and passive. He suggests suicide bombers, *committing such an act that incites fear … can be seen as acting out their own feelings of fear … In acting out, one does not deal directly with the emotions but behaves in a way consistent with these emotions, even if that behaviour is destructive to the self or others.*[60] He thought they rationalize these acts, hiding their deeper psychology.

Nasser Abufarha, a Palestinian ethnographer, studies his own culture from the inside, mapping the categories, beliefs, rituals and symbols that express or shape how its members interpret the world. In *The Making of a Human Bomb, an Ethnography of Palestinian Resistance*,[61] he describes how his own culture interprets and is shaped by the long conflict with Israel. He stresses that the word *istishhad*, meaning 'dying in martyrdom', has a quite different resonance from 'suicide bombing'. *Istishhad* is 'a cultural act loaded with meanings'. Using Durkheim's phrase 'altruistic suicide', he says the *istishhadi* offers his life as a sacrifice to the nation and land of Palestine.[62] Abufarha believes that *violent acts of martyrdom in Palestine … assert rootedness and identity among Palestinians, and resolve questions of denial and existence as well as uprooting and rootedness.*[63] Ragheb Jaradat blew up a bus, killing twenty-two Israelis as well as himself.[64] He wrote a note to his family: *Father hear me … Hear the echo of my voice … I am alive between the people … Fighting … in spite of my death … No I did not die … I now started living … Along with the beloved in heaven.*[65] Apart from the suggestion of reward in the afterlife for martyrdom, Abufarha highlights Jaradat's impact on this world after his death. He becomes an icon through sacrificing his body.

What is a suicide attack on a bus like? Here is an Israeli bystander's account of one. *I heard screaming, and I knew what had happened … I and a soldier broke open the front doors of the bus and bent the hot metal to create a hole for entry. We went in. Legs and arms without torsos were strewn everywhere … One man was still sitting in an upright position as if still on the bus, a cigarette box still bulging out of his shirt pocket. But part of his face and most of his brain were missing. He must be dead, I thought to myself, and turned instead to grab a woman's wrist dangling out of the blown-out bus window ... Desperately I shouted to her 'Do you have strength?' She raised her hand and opened her eyes, but the frenzy of rescuers ... made it impossible for me to get close enough to drag her out. I never saw her again.*[66] These things would not be justified even if all the victims had done bad things to Palestinians. Even for someone who disagrees, given the random nature of bus passengers, how could it possibly be right to kill them? Would babies or children on the bus deserve to die?

Abufarha's account is plausible about the culture and mindset of suicide bombers. But does he still have any *outside* perspective on their worldview? His account hovers between description and justification. The warm glow around becoming an icon through 'self-sacrifice' depends on blanking out the others killed. There is a revealing sentence (emphasis in the original): *'the victim, who is the istishhadi in the biological body, is the intermediary between the sacrificer (the istishhadi as the social person or in his or her identity) and those to whom the sacrifice is addressed, namely the land of Palestine, the Palestine place ...'.*[67] Perhaps the one clear thing in this blur of abstractions is leaving out the twenty-two other victims 'sacrificed' by Ragheb Jaradat.

Many Palestinians admire the suicide bombers, as *the best of our people, educated, successful.*[68] Some suicide bombers are educated and 'successful'. But the evidence is conflicting. After a prevented attack, interrogators on the spot could find them frightened, exhausted and confused. One said, *From the minute I put on the explosive belt, I thought how frightening it was but the situation was stronger than me. The more I kept going the more I hesitated.*[69] One former activist said that suicide terrorists were those who *walked next to the walls and are scared of their own shadow.*[70] Sometimes they keep their suicidal act in a separate compartment. One said his mission had to be on Monday, because on Tuesday he had a driving test.[71] Some in charge look down on suicide bombers. Sheikh Ahmad Yassin, after enthusiastically praising the quite small group of early bombers, could not remember the name or personal details of any of them.[72] Some said that, if their own children volunteered, they would prevent them.[73]

It is appalling to be a suicide bomber. It is morally worse to be a planner, persuading young people to kill horribly themselves and others. But leaders, too, are shaped by the cycle. When Abdul Rantisi was an infant, Israelis made his family flee to the Gaza Strip. When he was nine, Israeli soldiers killed his uncle. The adult Doctor Rantisi, a founder and leader of Hamas, was deeply involved in planning suicide bombings. First, he said, Hamas targeted only soldiers. But then Israeli police attacked Palestinian demonstrators at the Al-Aqsa Mosque, and during Ramadan Dr Baruch Goldstein massacred Palestinians in Hebron. From birth to death, Dr Rantisi's life was a miniature of the whole cycle. In 2004 the Israeli Air Force killed him by firing missiles at his car.

Killing in the Name of Anti-Terrorism[74]

Protection against terrorism is a main job of the Israeli security services. One director of Shin Bet, Ya'akov Peri, said the need for speed created pressure to do anything effective, including killing suspected terrorists.

In 1984 Palestinian terrorists hijacked a bus of Israeli passengers. The IDF stormed the bus. The two terrorists left alive were interrogated by Micha Kubi, a senior interrogator of Shin Bet. He described Avraham Shalom, the Director of Shin Bet, bringing down with all his strength the butt of a gun on the head of one terrorist so that it entered the skull. Shalom ordered the unit's commander, *Finish them off*. They were taken away and beaten to death with rocks and iron bars. Interviewed for Dror Moreh's documentary *The Gatekeepers*, Shalom said the two were beaten up by the army. *I authorized executing them, after they'd almost been beaten to death*. He accepted that killing them was wrong, but only if it became public. Asked about its morality, he said: *In the war on terror, forget morality. If you're dealing with a one-ton bomb, forget morality. There is no morality.*[75]

Terrorist suspects were sometimes reported missing by their families. When police asked Shin Bet if they knew anything, Yossi Ginossar said there was a standard response: they had no information: *We told the police every time they asked us, although we knew very well what hole he was buried in.*[76]

A terrorist about to kill is a legitimate target. Is it so different to kill planners further back in the chain? Israel's 'cutting off snakes' heads' response targeted those behind attacks. At least 1,000 people were killed in 500 targeted killings before the Second Intifada in 2000. During the intifada there were 168 such killings. Between 2000 and 2018, there were 400, roughly double the number by the United States (48 under President Bush and 353 under President Obama). *Every leader of Hamas and the Palestine Islamic Jihad was now a target. The plan was to kill them all.*[77] Israeli security services disrupted many terrorist attacks, but attempts increased. Ami Ayalon, a former director of Shin Bet, had doubts: *Drawing analogies between terrorism and a snake, which will stop functioning if you cut off its head, is such an oversimplification … Even if it does have a head, then it is an ideological head that hardly controls the operative head.*[78] Would this justify jihadists targeting Israel's Defence Minister? The Muslim Brotherhood's response was a substantial escalation of suicide bombings.

Torture

Most of us, including opponents of torture, have little idea of the nightmare it is. Jean Améry, tortured by the Nazis, started to tell us: *Torture is the most horrible event that a human being can retain within himself … they will do with me what they want … The boundaries of my body are also the boundaries of myself … At the first blow, however, this trust in the world breaks down … Twenty-two years later I am still dangling over the ground by dislocated arms … Whoever has succumbed to torture can no longer feel at home in the world.*[79]

Those who torture sometimes retreat behind its supposedly blurred boundaries. But, really, they are not so unclear: *For the purposes of this Convention, the term 'torture' means any act by which severe pain or suffering, whether physical or mental, is intentionally inflicted on a person for such purposes as obtaining from him or a third person information or a confession … inflicted by or at the instigation of or with the consent or acquiescence of a public official or other person acting in an official capacity.*[80]

Palestinian Security Services

The Palestinian Authority (PA) has its own security services, as does Hamas in Gaza. Drawing on 147 interviews covering eighty-six cases, Human Rights Watch investigated these services' methods. They found the PA and Hamas routinely torture critics and independent journalists. Dissent from the official line, whether on Israel or on the rival Palestinian group, risks the same treatment. Detainees are beaten, taunted and forced into painful stress positions for many hours. In 2017 at a PA detention centre in Jericho, Alaa Zaqeq was forced to half squat and later to stand on tiptoe with a rope pulling his arms towards the ceiling. In a detention in Gaza City, there was a room, 'the bus', where victims could be forced to sit on a small child's chair for hours or days. One felt *severe pain in my kidneys and spine*, as if his neck would break and his body was *tearing up inside*. Threats too are a nightmare. At the Jericho PA detention centre, Alaa Zaqeq was told he would leave in a wheelchair. A journalist, Sami As-Sai, who gave Hamas a list of Palestinian prisoners in Israeli prisons, was taken by PA forces to the detention centre, where he was told that sometimes people came with muscles and left without any. In Gaza, a man going into the bus for three days was told, *next time I will cause you a permanent disability.*

It is hard to disagree with the report by Human Rights Watch on the use of torture by the Palestinian Authority and by Hamas: *The habitual, deliberate, widely known use of torture, using similar tactics over years with no action taken by senior officials in either authority to stop these abuses, make these practices systematic. They also indicate that torture is governmental policy for both the PA and Hamas.*[81]

Israeli Security Services

The excuse afterwards is often 'a few rotten apples' did it, but the claim is suspect. Routine Israeli use of torture has been described by the late Avraham Shalom, a former director of the security service Shin Bet, and himself a suspect: *I once saw an interrogator kill an Arab. Not by beating him. He was throwing him from wall to wall, wall to wall, wall to wall*

... A week later the Arab died from a brain haemorrhage ... Everybody did it.[82]

And the 'few rotten apples' view is also rejected by Human Rights Watch: *Few of the abuses documented in this report are isolated occurrences. They are practiced with a considerable degree of consistency ... and with virtual impunity for the practitioners. The abuses are clearly being carried out with the knowledge of the government – although officials deny that the methods constitute torture.*[83]

Claims about Israeli torture overlap with Palestinian accounts. One report lists sleep deprivation, no food or hygiene; physical violence; being fixed in painful positions; extreme heat or cold; sensory deprivation; drugging; sexual harassment and humiliation; and threats of electric shocks. Many women had been locked in 'the coffin', a very dark room about a metre square so they could only stand or squat, with no toilet. One described four days there with sounds of a hissing snake and crying.[84] The 1994 report by Human Rights Watch/Middle East detailed three Palestinians who *died under interrogation in circumstances that indicate that interrogation and/or medical negligence directly or indirectly caused their death.* It includes a man who the Israeli authorities say hanged himself.

Euphemisms Inviting Complicity[85]

Avraham Shalom put it his way: *In the Netherlands, when a suspect doesn't confess, the interrogator leaves the room and comes back after about a week and says the same thing and comes back again after a week, and it goes on like that for a year. Over here, we slap him on the cheek and he talks; that's the whole difference.*

Slap him on the cheek: This account of Israeli interrogation hardly does justice to Avraham Shalom's own memories of someone being repeatedly thrown from wall to wall and dying of a brain haemorrhage. Ya'akov Peri's tenure as Shin Bet Director includes the period (1992–4) covered by the Human Rights Watch report. He says there is no torture in the security service, but there are *methods such as sleep deprivation, such as using expressions that are very far from diplomatic ... the atmosphere in the interrogation room is not that of a luxury hotel.*[86]

Expressions that are very far from diplomatic: Ya'akov Peri is of course right. It would be astonishing if interrogators put questions as diplomats might: 'With respect, I cannot but express some concern that your statement is not entirely complete'. *The atmosphere is not that of a luxury hotel.* Right again. No-one expects a room service menu or staff turning the bed down. The euphemisms try to blur such a dark reality. A Palestinian threat to cause you a permanent disability is not just un-diplomatic, like swearing. 'Not a luxury hotel' comes nowhere near the Palestinian 'bus' or the Israeli 'coffin'. Casual acceptance of these words is to become complicit in things impossible for decent people steadily to watch.

3

BREAKING THE CYCLE?

There is a Palestinian proverb: *Don't curse the darkness –*
light a candle.[1] The thought is echoed by the Israeli David
Kaposi in a book criticizing the covering of Gaza in parts
of the British press: *This, then, is the task that awaits those*
concerned with the discourse on Israel/Palestine and violence.
In place of the black and white of violent acts, the human
shades of grey ... in place of (physical or rhetorical) fighting,
that of dialogue and of understanding ... Understanding is
not a magic torch of divine proportions, only a flicker of
light in a dark room. Not necessarily able to bring the room
to light at once, but the only means by which the room does
not look very, very dark indeed.[2]

I: Glimpses of Light at the Dark Centre

People working in the dark parts of the cycle, including Shin
Bet leaders, sometimes glimpse its blindness and cruelty.
They include Ya'akov Peri: *You get to a house in the middle*
of the night, knock on doors, wake up a sleeping, cuddling
family. And the mother's tears, or the moment from parting
from that suspect you take from the arms of his family – are
not easy moments ... Those are the moments that ultimately
leave a deep impression on you. And when you retire from

the Service, you start leaning a bit to the left ... finally, seventy percent, eighty percent of the population ... wants to live in peace, to make a living, to feed itself, to feed its children ... And you start to feel some anger at the regime or the state that can't ultimately make an arrangement, reach an agreement ... which is what the majority on both sides want. Peri came to accept the conflict can be ended only by diplomacy, *by means of talking, of trust, of awareness of concessions, of compromise.*[3] Another Shin Bet director, Ami Ayalon, said humiliation and hopelessness may push a tractor driver to kill Israelis in a moment of anger. Shin Bet needs to look more at where it all comes from: *reading the surveys and reading the articles in the press and reading Amira Hass, and reading Palestinian poetry.*[4]

At the centre of the cycle are horrible acts of torture, targeted assassination and killing random groups of people. Among those there who have had glimpses of light about it, only Israelis have been quoted here. Despite less freedom to dissent, some Palestinians see the cycle for what it is and say so. They include public figures like Mahmoud Darwish and Sari Nusseibeh, and private citizens like Nonie Darwish. Hashim Abdul Raziq, Minister of Prisons for the Palestinian Authority, had been seventeen years in Israeli prisons. But, talking to Scott Atran, he said, *Do you think that I don't want peace? Do you think I want my son to suffer what I have suffered? Do you think that we are really that crazy?*[5]

It is not easy to find doubts expressed by Palestinians involved in terrorist bombing. But there is some evidence for them. In 2004, David Shulman reported seeing an Israeli news interview with senior prisoners from Hamas and Islamic Jihad. One had sent a terrorist to kill a family. *Astonishing sentences come from their mouths. They want peace; they want an agreement; they know what it will mean; they believe it is possible. It is wrong, says the arch-terrorist, to kill children – under any circumstances. He asks forgiveness of the father, who survived the shooting. In war, he says, children also get killed; it is wrong – nothing can justify it.*[6] There is a question about such statements. They could be made under pressure or in the hope of being released. But these 'astonishing sentences' are hardly more surprising than some of those made by Shin Bet directors. Perhaps the two groups should talk?

Perhaps nearly all Palestinians support suicide bombings. But it seems unlikely. Silence may also come from pressures not to speak. The plural voices loved in Israel are not encouraged. I would fear for any Palestinian group who spoke out against suicide bombing as the soldiers of *Breaking the Silence* speak out. Or self-censorship may come from Palestine being so much the conflict's loser, from not kicking your own side when it is down. And there may be cultural pressures. Roney Srour, a Palestinian clinician practising Western therapy, thinks many Palestinians' psychology may be shaped by how traditional Arab culture puts the needs of the family before the individual. There is little privacy. It may be hard to express emotions, so often kept private, in contrast to the more assertively individualist culture of Israelis.[7]

Extreme situations can destroy anti-Jewish stereotypes that support terrorism. Avraham Rivkind gave life-saving surgery to a captured terrorist. *I had seen the grisly results of his bus bombings ... Because I am a doctor, a believing Jew, a human being, I would never allow a patient to die whom I could save ... By filling the holes in their chests and bellies, I am making a statement that I am not like those forces of darkness that want to engulf this country in blood. Do they understand? I do not have the slightest doubt that they do. They thank me. They look at me differently. My people and I are no longer the demons of their ugly propaganda.*[8] This effect on one terrorist does not show that others without his experience can be reached. But even terrorists are human, reachable if a key to the human responses can be found.

Breakthrough as a Precursor of Peace?

The much more limited Northern Irish conflict stood comparison with Israel–Palestine for hostile stereotypes and mutual entrapment. The 1998 Good Friday Agreement created the (sadly, still fragile) peace of today. Many gradual steps led to it. One was the 1985 Hillsborough Agreement between Irish and British governments, creating an inter-governmental conference about Northern Ireland. Unionists disliked the role given to the Irish government. In debates in the United Kingdom Parliament, Unionist leaders forcefully expressed hostility. The Rev. Ian Paisley said the proposals were anathema to his constituents. *They want no part or lot in it, and they will not have it.* For himself, *I do not want to live under any system that is dominated by Roman Catholic social dogma.*[9] At that time the granite inflexibility was standard on both sides. But Paisley's speech contained a new note. He said the vast majority in Northern Ireland wanted peace. *I have followed too many funeral processions, I have held too many widows' hands ... not to know the agony my people have gone through. They are not only Protestant but Roman Catholic bereaved ones. I have received a lot of stick from Unionists for even going to their homes. I know what I am talking about. There is a desire for peace ... I am prepared to talk to the elected representatives of the people of Northern Ireland and to try to find some way whereby we can bring hope for a future when there will be something for our kids and young ones growing up ... I say that not because I need to say it but because it comes from my heart.*[10] Thirteen years later, Ian Paisley was famously pictured laughing and joking with Martin McGuiness of Sinn Fein after the Good Friday Agreement.

There are very good reasons for total rejection of both terrorist bombings and torture. But even bombers and torturers (and *even* those who order these things) may not be monsters. Some may be mainly decent people trapped into atrocities they wrongly think justified by what the other side does. Making peace may need seeing them – on both sides – as they are. There are signs of the human responses coming to some at the dark centre. As they think aloud about their mutual entrapment, peace may no longer seem quite so distant.

II: No Early Peace Deal: The Case of Oslo

Mahmoud Darwish caught something in his phrase ... *'between two small tribes adorned by the moonlight of two ancient faiths and an impossible peace'.*[11] But sometimes people do break out of seemingly intractable conflict.

Gorbachev (helped by Reagan and Thatcher) ended the Cold War. De Klerk ended apartheid by releasing Mandela.

Norway offered a secret channel for the stalled Israeli–Palestinian peace negotiations. There was a century of conflict to overcome. But both sides accepted. Israel needed secure borders and an end to intifada. The Prime Minister, Yitzhak Rabin, when Minister of Defence, had responded toughly to the First Intifada. But later he said he had come to see that you can't rule by force over one and a half million Palestinians. On the other side, Palestinians needed their own state, ending Israel's occupation and settlements. Each also hoped to end its isolation. In conversations between two leading negotiators, the PLO's Abu Ala (Ahmed Qurei) said to Israel's Uri Savir: *You'll give the key to the United States to us and we'll open the door of the Arab world to you.*[12]

The Palestinians had to overcome their own resistance. In theory Abu Ala wanted cooperation with Israel. *But I was very reluctant to sit together in a room with any Israeli.*[13] The Norwegian team were wonderful facilitators. They did not push for a 'Norwegian peace plan', but left the two sides to work out their own agreement. They were gently teasing in the introductions: 'Meet your Enemy Number One', etc.

There were serious disagreements and strong words. In one statement, Abu Ala summarized the problem: *Experience has taught us that our continued refusal to recognize the existence of Israel will not bring us the freedom we seek. On the other hand, your control over us has not brought you security and peaceful coexistence and cooperation.*[14] Uri Savir and Abu Ala came to see each other's commitment to peace. At first Abu Ala thought Uri Savir too tough in negotiation. But, walking in the forest, Uri Savir said to him: *I have felt ashamed of representing a state that is occupying the territory of others. I want the country to which I belong, and of which I am proud, to bring to an end the shame of occupation, and to live at peace with its neighbours. I wish to live in a democratic country that respects others and is respected by them.*[15] This changed Abu Ala. He said to Uri Savir that *even when negotiations get rough, we both agree that we must make a better future for our children. Let's dedicate our speeches to each other's children.*[16] Friendship evolved. Uri Savir remembered Abu Ala first calling him by his first name: *You know, Uri, I have the feeling we can bring this off.* He replied, *So do I.*[17]

It was not only negotiators who felt hope and history might rhyme. So did the Director of Shin Bet, Ya'akov Peri. *You're meeting people who were definitely part of the other side for the first time. It's a shock. But when both sides come truly meaning to try and reach an agreement ... the feeling is that it's possible and that there's a huge responsibility on your shoulders. You really feel the rush of history's wings.*[18] Meeting one particular Palestinian made a special impact. Through Shin Bet's work, Jibril Rajoub had been imprisoned from the age of sixteen. Now on the Fatah Central Committee, he *had the ability to break the ice with little stories and things that showed that ... we might be on different sides of the line, but his knowledge of us and our knowledge of them ... is amazing. And you see you're ultimately meeting human beings whose desire for peace, whose desire for quiet, equal yours.*[19] There were of course great difficulties. The teams did not have a free hand. Israeli delegates had Rabin at the other end of the phone. The PLO delegates had Arafat on another line.

Justice and the Imbalance of Power

The two teams worked in an atmosphere of equality, but with very unequal power. Abu Ala had to accept Uri Savir's tough statement: *Jerusalem is the focus of Israel's national spirit, and if its status is subject to negotiation, we will be unable to achieve any progress.*[20] No Palestinian refusal would have been so decisive.

Uri Savir's and Abu Ala's accounts are together a classic of the literature of peace-making. Growing mutual trust helped compromise. There are interesting asides. Israel and Palestine *each* saw themselves as David against Goliath. And (on both sides) *We don't like you because you remind us of ourselves.*[21] Some beliefs were given up. Uri Savir found Israel's 'enlightened occupation' was a myth. *A West Bank Palestinian could not build, work, study, purchase land, grow produce, start a business, take a walk at night, enter Israel, go abroad, or visit his family in Gaza or Jordan without a permit from us.* Israelis who had ruled over Palestinians found it hard to treat them as equals, saying *We have decided to allow you to do* this or that.[22]

Negotiations could be overwhelmed by Palestinian distress and anger about checkpoint searches and other humiliations. Abu Ala said, *We're prepared to move closer to your position ... But I will not agree to the degradation of my people. You, here, I trust. But tomorrow some officer or border policeman may come along with a yen to torment Palestinians.* To one Israeli who mentioned interrogating suspects in a sterile area: *You relate to our people like animals!*[23] Palestinian reaction to Israeli toughness could bring results. Abu Ala said: *You want full responsibility for security, but you won't grant us full civil jurisdiction. You won't recognize our national rights. The settlements are to remain intact. And you call this self-rule? It's nothing but the continuation of occupation by other means!*[24] Uri Savir replied: *We will not yield on security for Israelis. We will not make you responsible for it. We have been fighting for a century. We're just now beginning to build mutual trust.*[25] Abu Ala said: *We were prepared to make significant compromises. But I don't see the point in going on any longer ... I don't blame anyone, but I have nothing more to contribute ... I have decided to resign from the talks.*[26] Later Uri Savir went alone and made (unauthorized) proposals that brought him back.

For the agreement Israel had made some real concessions, including withdrawal from the Golan Heights, important for their defence. But, overall, Israel held more of the cards. A reason Uri Savir gave for not discussing Jerusalem was that it was 'the focus of Israel's national spirit'. The *effective* reason was the other one: include Jerusalem and we will get nowhere. Having more to lose, the Palestinians accepted the exclusion. It *is* unfair when the stronger party has this kind of dominance.

John Rawls saw a just society in terms of a thought experiment. He imagined rational self-interested people negotiating about a future society under important constraints. In real-world negotiations the rich might support low taxes and the poor support generous welfare. The thought experiment aims to eliminate such bias. His imagined negotiators are in the 'original position': not knowing the place in society they will occupy. But this leaves it unclear *what* they will choose. Gamblers might want billionaires, betting they will be among them. Insurance-minded people might fear they would be poor and press for generous welfare. Influenced by negotiators' psychology, the thought experiment may not produce agreed results.[27]

But Rawls' model is still a very rough guide to what is just. If each of the Oslo negotiators had (with impossible ignorance) not known whether they were Palestinians or Israelis, the results would have been different. The actual results did not fit Rawlsian justice. In Rawls' original position, the impossibly ignorant negotiators might see that each nation would need the security demanded by real-world Israelis. They might also see that, as a minimum, each nation would need a genuinely independent state. If these are incompatible, negotiations might collapse. On a more optimistic view, they might have sacrificed pure justice to come up with some compromise, giving each nation less than they wanted, but still quite a lot. In messy world negotiations, results are often disputed. Away from the pure air of the original position, the price of agreement is often unfairness. Negotiations would very rarely take place if parties always had to have equal strength. And unequal power tilts outcomes towards the stronger. Excluding Jerusalem was unfair, as was the failure to agree a unitary independent Palestinian state. For Edward Said the result for Palestinians was *a series of ... reservations or Bantustans separated by Israeli roads and settlements except in the north.*[28]

They did reach an agreement. The gains for each side were unequal but still real. Israel and the PLO recognized each other. The PLO would respect Israel's need for security. Israel would withdraw from Gaza, and from Ramallah, Jericho and other West Bank cities. It would recognize limited Palestinian self-rule. The missing bits make Oslo a most implausible permanent settlement. And, however this agreement might be improved, there would remain the conflict between Israel and Hamas. Oslo is far from the best imaginable. But, if seen as an early move towards a two-state solution, it was still good. Results are rarely more than partly just, but can still help towards peace. So, not three cheers for Oslo, but perhaps one.

Though, if followed up in the right way, perhaps two? Abu Ala thought: *The spirit of the Oslo Agreement could still carry within it the promise of a new relationship between Israel and Palestine. It could still provide a peaceful substitute for the existing state of confrontation, suffering and bloodshed.*[29] And Uri Savir thought: *The Passover Hagaddah we read every year to celebrate our liberation from slavery in ancient Egypt includes a song that reminds us: 'In every generation [our enemies] rise up to destroy us, and the Almighty saves us from their hand.' This song the Jews have sung for centuries and still do. Yet at the end of the twentieth century, the leaders of the State of Israel acted on the promise that enemies may not be eternal; that we may be strong enough to transform them into partners.*[30]

But Raja Shehadeh despaired: *After secret negotiations in Oslo, an agreement was reached between Israel and the PLO ... The occupied territories were divided into three areas, with Israel retaining full control of the settlements. There was no insistence on a settlement freeze ... As the negotiations were proceeding for a final agreement more settlements were being built and existing ones expanded at a faster pace than ever, doubling the number of settlers in the West Bank. It took several years before people were able to grasp the disaster that was the Oslo Accords.*[31]

Hopes Killed

A poll after Rabin returned from signing the Oslo Agreement suggested 81 per cent of Israelis supported it.[32] But opponents on both sides started to erode support. Uri Savir remembered Abu Ala often saying that, if you obtain agreements that the public deems unfair, they will not hold.[33] There was a Palestinian 'rejectionist' front against the agreement.[34] Six of the eighteen-member PLO Executive Committee resigned. Hamas ran a terror campaign to provoke Israeli opposition to Oslo. Two Israeli hikers in the West Bank were brutally killed, suggesting that the PLO could not deliver its side of the deal.

There were passionate Israeli opponents. Before talks were concluded a religious settler, Dr Baruch Goldstein, massacred 29 Muslims at prayer in Hebron. He was then killed. His motives probably went beyond revenge for Muslim attacks to turning Palestinians away from the peace deal. Opponents on both sides had a common aim.[35] Responding to the massacre, a Hamas suicide bomber blew up a car full of explosives in an Israeli town, killing eight people. In Goldstein's home settlement, people were threatened not to criticize the massacre. The grave there was a shrine.

In Israel the National Religious Party called withdrawing from Gaza and Jericho treachery. The Likud leader, Binyamin Netanyahu, said the government was letting the PLO destroy Israel. Uri Savir was given a bodyguard when his name appeared on a settlers' blacklist. A kidnapped Israeli soldier was killed when the rescue operation went wrong. The crowd at a demonstration shouted 'This peace is killing us' and 'Rabin is a murderer'. Many religions have a dark side. But the journalist Avigdor Eskin carried out against Rabin what must be one of the most hate-filled religious ceremonies: the Pulsa diNura, in which angels are asked to prevent any forgiveness of someone's sins so that they experience all the Biblical curses and then die.[36] Mainstream Judaism rejects this, forbidding praying for someone's death.

Binyamin Netanyahu was at demonstrations where crowds chanted 'Death to Rabin'. The anti-Oslo demonstrators likened Rabin to Pétain, the French collaborator with the Nazis. There were pictures of him with blood on his hands. At one demonstration a mock funeral of Rabin took place with a hangman's noose over the coffin, on which was written 'Murderer of Zionism'. Netanyahu walked between the coffin and the noose. Another demonstration with Netanyahu in the grandstand included an effigy of Rabin in SS uniform. There seems something dark about a mental climate in which someone thought fit to be Prime Minister could be involved in such events. Carmi Gillon, then head of Shin Bet, says he used the word 'murder' when he warned Netanyahu and others: *Listen, when you're talking from the balcony in Zion Square, I can't imagine that you have any idea what could happen, you're certainly not supporting it, but it could happen.*[37]

Gillon talked similarly to religious leaders. Three respected rabbis wrote an opinion suggesting a collision between Judaism and the Jewish state. They thought taking part in Israeli evacuations under the peace agreement (leaving the Golan Heights, Gaza and parts of the West

Bank) was forbidden for a Jew. Maimonides was cited: *Even if the King orders you to violate the Laws of the Torah, it is forbidden to obey.* In one poll 18 per cent of Israelis thought soldiers should follow their rabbis, not their orders.[38] In a letter to forty 'wise men' of Judaism, three settler rabbis went much further. Citing the rise in terrorist attacks on settlers since Oslo, they asked whether Rabin and his government were accomplices to terrorist murder of Jews. Should they be tried? If guilty, what should their sentences be?

Yigal Amir was a religious zealot influenced by this climate. He accepted Judaism's doctrine of *din rodef*: a bystander is allowed to save the life of an innocent person by killing a murderous *rodef* (pursuer). Without seeing *himself* as a murderous pursuer, he believed the doctrine obliged him to kill Rabin. After speaking at a huge peace rally, Rabin was about to get into his car. Amir shot him. Arrested and interrogated, Amir made it clear that he considered the murder justified. Chillingly, in the interrogation room he asked for a schnapps so that he could toast Rabin's death.

The murderous climate led to other celebrations. Years later, Ami Ayalon as Director of Shin Bet dismissed a man from the Prime Minister's security team because he had danced when Rabin was murdered. The man protested: *It was a burst of joy; what could we do?* His parents said: *Our whole community was dancing. The threat of withdrawing from the Golan Heights had been removed.* Ami Ayalon said: *Can you hear what you're saying? Do you listen to yourselves?*[39]

The new Prime Minister, Shimon Peres, was determined to implement the Oslo Agreement. There seemed a good chance that he would win the election. During the campaign Hamas terrorist attacks on Jerusalem caused many deaths. Netanyahu's support grew and Peres' lead faded. Netanyahu narrowly won. Fanatical Israelis and Palestinians had known how each other were likely to react. Baruch Goldstein may have wanted his massacre to stir up Hamas against the agreement. Hamas murdered the hikers to fan Israeli opposition to it. They hated each other but together succeeded. The Oslo Agreement was dead.

III: Cooperation?

The fate of Oslo suggests pessimism about further attempts at an early end to the conflict. Could piecemeal cooperation on specific issues be a better strategy? But, with so little mutual trust, can this be more successful?

Axelrod: Tit-for-Tat

In 1984 Robert Axelrod published *The Evolution of Cooperation*, about rational and purely self-interested people or groups in conflict with each other.[40] Is cooperation between them possible?

Game theory gave reason to doubt it. When two people play Prisoners' Dilemma against each other, each has to choose either DEFECT or COOPERATE, without knowing the other's choice. They do know the way the rewards for different outcomes are stacked. Taking them both together, their joint best result comes only when they both choose COOPERATE. But things are stacked so that, *whichever* choice one makes, the other will do better by choosing DEFECT. So rational self-interested players will always both choose DEFECT, giving a worse joint result. (This discouraging outcome rests on those ways of stacking the rewards. *How* discouraging depends on how many real cases reflect this pattern.)

Axelrod asked if the apparent disaster for rational self-interested cooperation could be escaped. His research on Prisoners' Dilemma had a single addition. No game was a one-off. The players knew each was part of an extended series. Axelrod invited suggestions for strategies that might do best in the series.

The winning strategy was TIT-FOR-TAT. Choose cooperate in the first game. After that, respond to the opponent's move in the previous game. Cooperate to reward the opponent's cooperation. Defect to punish the opponent's defection. Players confronting TIT-FOR-TAT can see that the best results for both will come only if they cooperate. This study is encouraging even about cases where rewards reflect the Prisoners' Dilemma pattern. The benefits of future cooperation can make it rational for purely self-interested groups to build mutual trust rather than take the immediate reward for defection.

Those who study particular conflicts sometimes question the easy transfer of abstract game theory to real-world peace-keeping. William Ian Miller, an authority on blood-feuds in medieval Iceland, points out that a series of Prisoner's Dilemma games can be isolated from anything else in partici-pants' lives. But real policy-makers may be playing several games at once, using the same 'move' to send different messages to different people.[41]

In the Israel–Palestine conflict, it is plausible to see cooper-ation and peace as by far the best outcome for each. Does this mean that, if they are rational, they will give up short-term gains for the joint long-term benefits of mutual trust? Possibly, but not certainly. As well as the 'multiple messages' complication, there are factors that disrupt rational self-interested cooperation.

One disrupter is the very unequal power of the two sides. The best outcome for both might be a Palestinian state on the West Bank, with the settlements removed, the Golan Heights as part of secure Israeli borders, and mutually respectful sharing of Jerusalem. Many Palestinians might see this as so much better than where they are now: a chance not to be missed. But many Israelis, not wanting to give up the settle-ments, might think that their side's much greater military and economic power allows them to impose an outcome more in their interests. They could, *perhaps* rationally, deny that for *them* cooperation and peace are best.

A second disrupter comes from the cycle of violence. Bitterness could make each reject a deal greatly benefitting both, rather than make the needed concessions. Cycles of violence can turn rational game-players into something quite different.

Even between two equally powerful sides who had put bitterness behind them, there would be a third disrupter. Among both Palestinians and Israelis, there are groups with values they see as non-negotiable. Those who believe God promised the Jews a greatly expanded Israel may value this more than any peace. Palestinians who believe Allah said Jews cannot be trusted and should be killed may think this more important than peace. To put it mildly, these particular beliefs are open to question. But, for those holding them, the *choices* are not irrational. These poorly based beliefs may weaken. But now they are obstacles to TIT-FOR-TAT strategies and so to peace.

Netanyahu once told Syrians and Palestinians to concentrate on economic relations rather than sovereignty. But the Syrian Foreign Minister put first non-negotiable values: *sovereignty over land is the key to this region, because it is for Arabs a question of honour and dignity.*[42] Perhaps progress depends on *first* addressing concerns that may be economically 'irrational', but psychologically deeper.

Cooperation over Water?

Shared projects still help. Small-scale peace groups bring together people of good will to get to know each other. Large-scale projects involving politicians and business people may be very important, as they were in Northern Ireland. Politicians on both sides, sometimes barely speaking to each other, had to construct a bid for European regional funds. Sharing hopes and plans on the flight to Brussels is said to have changed how they talked to each other about the conflict. Can there be large Israeli–Palestinian projects? Might some be about water? They are certainly needed.[43]

The river Jordan is the large shared source. Before the Six-Day War, moves to divert the river threatened Israel's supply. The war gave Israel control over the West Bank water sources. Few Palestinian villages there have piped water. Israel restricts Palestinian drilling of wells. Israeli settlers use around three times more water than Palestinians in the West Bank. Palestinians are only weakly involved in decisions. They may not understand different overlapping military orders and are reluctant to cooperate with the civil authority. Using relatively little water, they often do not prevent pollution.

Cooperation over water gets urgency from population density. Both sides have competed to have the larger population. After centuries of Jews being a discriminated-against minority, Israel's first Prime Minister Ben Gurion said that only a state with at least 80 per cent Jews is a stable

Jewish state.[44] Golda Meir when Prime Minister said she feared waking wondering how many Arab babies had been born in the night.[45] The Palestinian Red Crescent Society sees high Palestinian fertility as a sign of their nation's continued existence. Population (in Israel, the West Bank and Gaza) rose from about half a million around 1900 to about 14 million in 2019. In one of the world's most densely populated regions, with limited water, how can the absurd competition to have the larger population be replaced?

Needing water can help. The 1994 Jordan–Israel Peace Treaty included agreement on water. It was based on the principle (monitored by a joint water committee) that each side will ensure that it does not harm the other's water resources. Can Israel and Palestine follow this? Because of their interdependence, they both lose by non-cooperation. In the Oslo II Interim Agreement, Israel recognized Palestinian water rights in the West Bank and agreed a joint Water Commission. In 2001, Israel and the Palestinian Authority made a joint statement calling on Jews and Palestinians to respect their intertwined water infrastructure. Bernard Wasserstein said that where resource competition endangers both sides, they will recede from a zero-sum game and instead decide to cooperate. We may hope he was right. But the optimism assumes both sides are rational game-players. This has some support. But history is a warning. Irrational groups who hate each other can combine to kick over the table.

IV: Solutions? Or Starting a Conversation?

An acceptable solution should pass a difficult 'double-double' test. It has to ensure the essential combination of both self-determination and security for both Palestinians and Israelis.

A dismaying response suggests itself to accounts of the major alternative 'solutions', two states or a shared single state. Those supporting two states are at their most convincing about why a single state is unrealizable and/or unworkable. Single-state supporters are at their most convincing about why two states are unrealizable and/or unworkable. Neither gives a problem-free account of their own solution.

One-State Solutions

Both Israelis and Palestinians, thinking about a shared single state, are likely to fear and reject minority status. At any given time, one people will be outnumbered. Few Palestinians who have lived under Israeli occupation can welcome a single democratic state with an Israeli majority. In Israel itself, Judaism has a protected status not given to Islam. Does the Palestinian minority in Israel really feel they have equality with the Jewish majority? Benny Morris probably speaks for many Israelis in doubting that a single state with a Palestinian majority would allow freedom to Judaism. He cited Muslim persecution of Christians. *Western liberals like or pretend to view Palestinian Arabs, or indeed all Arabs, as Scandinavians.*[46]

Some accounts of a single state try to meet these points by proposing constitutionally entrenched guarantees of the rights of both peoples. But 'entrenched' guarantees can be overturned. One main point of Zionism, as Herzl saw it, was not to rely on such things.

Two-State Solutions

A two-state solution seems to give each people a better chance of self-determination and of safety from each other. In the abstract it may be possible to design a version (*very* roughly) just to both. But, for each people, the gap between that and what they care about is so huge.

One relatively plausible two-state version was outlined in an agreement proposed in 2003 by Sari Nusseibeh and Ami Ayalon. Permanent frontiers would be based on the 1967 borders, and include a Palestinian link between the West Bank and the Gaza strip. Jerusalem would be an open city, with religious freedom and access for all to the holy sites. It would be the capital of two states. Jews would have the 'right of return' only to the State of Israel and Palestinians only to the State of Palestine. The international community would guarantee the security of a de-militarized Palestine.

This proposal would struggle for support on either side. There would be great Israeli resistance to losing the settlements and part of what some see as a Greater Israel. Amos Oz pointed out Israel's extra security risk from future Arab attacks launched from Palestine, and how much the Palestinians would lose of what was once theirs: *Goodbye Haifa, Goodbye Jaffa, Goodbye Beer Sheva ... This is going to hurt like hell.*[47] To expect the Palestinians to sign away all this without huge gains in return seems wishful thinking.

Federal and Semi-Federal Solutions

In the late 1960s the Israeli peace activist Uri Avnery suggested a model emerging from a two-state solution. A newly created Palestinian state would join Israel in a federation. Avnery proposed a next stage: a 'Semitic Union', a confederacy of all the states in the region.[48] This retains the unpalatability to both sides of the two-state solution. And, leaving aside frictions between Arab states, would there be much support for a Semitic Union in either Palestine or Israel?

A more plausible solution might be driven by ecology. The water issue shows how national boundaries may not track a shared ecological region. Omar Dahbour suggests a federation in response.[49] Federation need not be all-or-none. The best solution may contain a variety of different overlapping sovereignties. Cooperation expressed sometimes in blurred or shared control helped in the Israel–Jordan agreement on water. Limited and local cooperation over specific shared problems do not arouse the hostile passions that first limited and then killed the Oslo Agreement.

Those hostile passions: do people really *want* a way out? Ludwig Wittgenstein: *What is your aim in philosophy? To show the fly the way out of the fly-bottle.* What if the bottle contains two flies, fighting each other so furiously they have no interest in the way out? But Israelis, Palestinians and the rest of us are not flies but thinking humans who can talk to each other. Amos Oz did not expect to see peace in his lifetime. He said it will take many years, the hatred and fear being so deep. But he believed we should trust the enemy and they have to become trustworthy in our eyes. That all sounds far away. But it still may be our best hope.

'Thou and Thou Comprising We': From Solutions To Conversation

Within a Place, not of Names,
But of Personal Pronouns,
Where I hold council with Me
And recognise as present
Thou and Thou comprising We,
... No voice is raised in quarrel,
But quietly We converse ...
W.H. AUDEN: *Aubade*

It may be good to turn from ever-receding 'solutions', and try by a thousand small steps slowly to shuffle away from war. Conversation can help, especially if it includes deeper values on both sides. The aim could be Oz's: for each to become trustworthy in the other's eyes. This will alarm many Palestinians, fearing that by 'peace' Israeli governments mean Palestinians ceasing to resist, while Israel keeps everything it has. Anyone who reads the next chapter of this book will find that here conversation is not just verbal, but includes non-violent resistance. Perhaps some Israelis, reading that, will stop reading this book. But would they really reject 'I and Thou' conversations?

Many varied conversations could help people on both sides move further away from the conflict's mindsets. The big drawback is how slowly deeply embedded outlooks change. Progress, although real, will be slow. But the cycle of violence has made them so mutually distrustful: why choose slow conversations? Pessimism may be right. But there are hopeful signs, some glimpses of light at the dark centre. And a probable Israeli–Palestinian shared hope. Suppose two babies, one Palestinian, one Israeli, are born on the same day. If their families were asked, 'Do you think in twenty years' time they will be trying to kill each other?' the answer might be 'Oh, please not'. Perhaps even very slow progress is better than none?

4

JOINING THE
CONVERSATION
OF MANKIND

The phrase was Michael Oakeshott's. *The Voice of Poetry in the Conversation of Mankind* was the title of an essay in which he said that *the diverse idioms of utterance which make up current human intercourse have some meeting-place ... the image of this meeting-place is not an inquiry or an argument but a conversation ... begun in the primeval forests and extended and made more articulate in the course of centuries.*[1] His ghost deserves an apology. I like his phrase 'the conversation of mankind' and what it stands for. His civilized and engaging discussion of it was more abstract, more subtle, than mine. Oakeshott's conversation was between different ways of imagining, expressed in many different 'voices', including those of science, of practical affairs and of poetry.

His ideas can be hard to keep in focus. How do we recognize a voice? What should we listen for when a voice is heard? Which activities have their own voice? Are there voices of motherhood, of poverty, of old age, of religion? How dominant are his three voices? Here they are ignored (apart from, briefly, poetry). Less subtle features are audible. He might have regretted this attempt to put his subtle idea to unsubtle use. But the hope is to escape from loud, defensive-aggressive talk, from conflict to conversation.

Conversations have freedom to range, not to be restricted by some organizing person. Here no definition of 'conversation' is given but the conversation of *peace* is central. That excludes threats or other coercion. The unwelcome chat with the blackmailer is not the model. A message was communicated by the atom bomb on Hiroshima. Even if it ended the war, it was no opening gambit in the conversation of peace.

Good topics in the conversation of mankind include exploring conflict and peace-making. The South African struggle against apartheid was followed by work towards reconciliation. From Northern Ireland's peace-making, things can be learnt about international help, and about not segregating education on religious or tribal lines. The dark cycle for and against jihad is cousin to the Israel–Palestine cycle. A school in what was once the French 'capital of jihad' may have lessons for its cousin.

I: Conversation Across the Divide and Across the Globe

Not all cooperation is about solutions. It can be more psychological: not turning a deaf ear when an opponent expresses a justifiable concern, or suddenly seems to be speaking from the heart. It can start by avoiding denial: accepting that horrible things are done by 'our' side as well as theirs, accepting that 'they' too do good things. After Jewish doctors saved her brother's life, Nonie Darwish was brave to say that in that time of crisis an Arab could trust Jews. When IDF soldiers bravely went public about horrors in the West Bank, they were 'Breaking the Silence'. Few things could be more liberating for both Israelis and Palestinians than breaking down the barriers of denial. The hope is that one day Arabs and Jews together will celebrate the brave people, Israelis and Palestinians, who first broke the silence.

Conversation need not revolve around conflict. Daniel Barenboim and Edward Said founded the West-Eastern Divan Orchestra. Since Said's death, Barenboim still leads it. This conversation was about music (with a hint of politics?).[2]

EDWARD SAID: One feels that certain things are irrecoverable because they are past. In the Berg Concerto, in the final movement, the appearance of the Bach Chorale is profoundly moving, precisely because it's so at odds with the material presented there ... because of the glaring contrast between the two. Surely you feel that as well, don't you, even with Beethoven?

DANIEL BARENBOIM: *I'm actually bothered by the Bach Chorale ... Somehow it introduces a foreign element into ... the piece.*

E.S: But what if you were told by him ... 'Well, I intended it'?

D.B: *Yes, I'm sure. Well, I'm still bothered by it.*

E.S. The bother, itself, is what I'm interested in. I mean, that could also be a part of the aesthetic experience: those jarring messages that come in and disrupt what could be a utopian, ideal situation.

D.B: *I think that the most wonderful thing about the aesthetic experience of music ... is that you go from one to the other ... from angularity to roundness, from masculinity to femininity ... from heroic to lyric, all these things. And ... to learn to live with that is to learn to live with the fluidity of life. You must have the courage to accept the fluidity of elements that happens in development. Every development, every departure, means leaving something behind.*

E.S: No. I disagree with that. I really think that there are certain things that one mustn't accept. And for me ... Beethoven is, to a certain extent, about that. That is to say, there is a resistance. In other words, I don't think everything can be resolved.

D.B: *Of course not.*

(Barenboim has said, *It is absolutely essential for people ... to understand what the other thinks and feels, without necessarily agreeing with it ... I want to ... create a platform where the two sides can disagree and not resort to knives.*)

The Palestine–Israel conversation can be about shared values. In 2003, teachers and students publicly defended Al-Quds University. Professor David Shulman of the Hebrew University of Jerusalem spoke at Al-Quds. *We are here to protest against the attack on Al-Quds University, the seizure of a large part of the University's lands in the interests of building the so-called Separation Fence or Wall. For a thousand years ... the institution of the university has embodied certain basic values – human dignity, respect for the other and his or her dignity, tolerance, freedom of thought and expression, unfettered curiosity, and the rejection of all forms of violence and coercion. Let there be no mistake: an attack on a university is an attack upon these key concepts. It is our simple human duty to stand here and protest when such an attack is imminent. Al-Quds University and the Hebrew University are sisters ... they share a vision and a set of values ... We stand beside you, we will not be silent, we will face these dangers together, we will not give up on the hope of peace.*[3]

'A Decent Respect to the Opinions of Mankind'

The United States Declaration of Independence says: *When in the Course of human events, it becomes necessary for one people to dissolve the political bonds which have connected them with another ... a decent respect to the opinions of mankind requires that they should declare the causes which impel them to the separation ...* It continues: *We hold these truths to be self-evident, that all men are created equal ...* We now see, as Thomas Jefferson did not, the obvious question about owning slaves. But 'a decent respect to the opinions of mankind' still reverberates.

Mankind's opinions are rarely unanimous, so it may turn into respecting the opinions that mankind *should* hold, or that *decent* people do hold. The decent opinions of mankind are often ignored: by Putin, but many others too. Saudi Arabia sanctions the stoning to death of women. And supported by the United States and Britain, it wages a cruel war in Yemen. Iran wages the same cruel war. Britain joined the 2003 invasion of Iraq. It is deeply implicated in the arms trade, including the cruelties in Yemen. A United States administration created a concentration camp where some people were tortured that had been kidnapped by their forces. China threatens Taiwan, breaks treaty obligations to preserve Hong Kong democracy, and 're-educates' huge numbers of Muslims in concentration camps. Syria, Belarus, Myanmar, Iran, Afghanistan ... The list is no reason to stop demanding a decent respect to the opinions of mankind.

In 2020, Binyamin Netanyahu's government, encouraged by President Donald Trump, planned the illegal annexation of parts of the occupied territories. This caused concern among many in the Jewish diaspora. On perhaps the reasonable grounds that it did not take sides in Israeli politics, the Board of Deputies of British Jews did not condemn the proposal. But over forty distinguished British Jews did protest to the Israeli ambassador. They said their concerns were shared by *large numbers of the British Jewish community, including many in its current leadership, even if they choose not to express them ... We have yet to see an argument that convinces us, committed Zionists and passionately outspoken friends of Israel, that the proposed annexation is a constructive step ... it would ... be a Pyrrhic victory intensifying Israel's political, diplomatic and economic challenges without yielding any tangible benefit. It would have grave consequences for the Palestinian people most obviously. Israel's international standing would also suffer.*[4]

II: Non-Violent Resistance as Communication

Among the reasons for Palestinians to choose non-violent resistance, two stand out.

One was given by Yuval Diskin, Head of Israel's security service Shin Bet from 2005 to 2011: *If the Palestinians had adopted not a line of terrorist attacks but a line of non-violent resistance, it would have created much larger problems for us than the attacks. The suicide attacks weakened the legitimacy of the battle.*[5]

The other was given by Lucy, a Palestinian woman from near Bethlehem: *I started my life not believing in non-violent resistance. At a certain point* [the Second Intifada] *I decided, 'No. I have to stop. This is not going to change.' Arms just lead to bloodshed and revenge, no more than this. I felt that using arms is not going to achieve anything – just to see more blood, more victims. This was the most important part for me. That's why I promised myself to be an active person in the field of peace-making ... to educate people to raise their awareness of the effect of non-violence.*[6]

Budrus

Palestinians have resisted, sometimes violently, what they see as colonial occupation. The (mainly peaceful) First Intifada did include stone-throwing. From 2000, after a decade of increasing settlements, the Second Intifada was much more violent. But some like Lucy (above) reacted against it. Palestinian non-violent resistance came from villages harmed by Israeli decisions. In 2003, bulldozers were sent to Budrus, a village near the 'Green Line' frontier with Israel, to clear land for the Separation Wall. The planned route would divide the cemetery and overshadow the school, encircling Budrus and five other villages. It would destroy the villagers' livelihood, taking from them 300 acres and 3,000 olive trees.

Non-violent Protest: Inclusiveness

Ten months of non-violent protest were led by Ayed Morrar. It was strikingly inclusive. Peace activists came from South Africa, the United States and other countries. Morrar appreciated especially the Israelis. *When we started struggling in Budrus, we didn't imagine that we can find this number of Israeli friends to support us. That's like a dream.*[7] The campaign worked by including all political parties. Some from other countries questioned the Hamas flags. Morrar replied: *you have to accept Hamas flags too, because we consider it an accomplishment to get them to participate in a peaceful act.*[8]

It reflected the friendly relations between Morrar and Ahmed Awwad, a local Hamas-supporting teacher. On each side there was some calculation. Awwad was not committed to non-violence, but thought it good tactics. Violence would let the IDF see them as terrorists and use all their weapons. Morrar said, *I think I may be the most ardent critic of the ideology of Hamas*, but he saw them as part of Palestinian society and able to sabotage what they rejected. Two different outlooks, but in Budrus, non-violent together.

Involving women was rare. Morrar's 15-year-old daughter, Iltezam, was key to this: *I noticed that at first it was only men ... I asked my dad, 'How come there are only men in the marches? I think women also have to be there. Are you taking women with you?' He replied, 'Today, no. But tomorrow everybody is welcome'.* Later he said several times as many women as men took part. The soldiers found it harder to be violent to women. In the documentary *Budrus* (made by the

Brazilian director Julia Bacha), Iltezam said she saw *the men trying to push the soldiers and none of them could do that. But* (smiling) *I think the girls could do it.* Iltezam herself was a leader of the women. They often reached the bulldozers first and lay down in front of them. It took courage. The danger was real. *About 300 people were injured with rubber bullets or through inhaling tear gas.* Iltezam did not disguise the fear she had to overcome. *I said to myself. OK I will not be afraid. But when I first see the army, I do indeed feel fear … They might hit you, shoot you or imprison you.* One time she jumped into the hole a bulldozer was going towards. *I asked myself, what can one person do? I jumped in the hole. I was completely terrified. The soldier could do nothing except taking the bulldozer and going away.*

How Some Participants Saw Things

In the documentary *Budrus*, Ayed Morrar was interviewed, as were the IDF officer Captain Doron Spielman and his Border Police colleague Yasmine Levy. During the protest, Yasmine Levy was given a hard time by the Palestinian women, who teased her, 'Yasmine, come and join us', offering to find her a nice Palestinian man: She did not do so and later ordered tear gas to be used. But she also showed understanding of the villagers' case. *When I arrived, there were still olive trees, which for them are as valuable as life. We were given clear instructions not to damage what was valuable to them. But when there was no choice but to put up the fence they brought in the bulldozers.* While holding to her view that the wall was essential, her respect for the Palestinian women grew. *Even if the women were beaten up or hit by rubber bullets or stun grenades, they had no problem with it. They went to all lengths to ensure their land would remain theirs.* She still accepted tough measures could be needed. *When the negotiation didn't work, we got orders to use more aggressive tactics to push them back because the work had to continue.*

Captain Spielman argued that the villagers were not the only people whose lives were at risk. In two years, hundreds of Israelis had been killed in terrorist attacks that the wall was meant to stop. He had to obey his orders to ensure it was built. But, within that framework, he was concerned to do as little as possible to violate the villagers' rights. Later he said: *Ultimately, a non-violent protest is not going to stop the way of the fence. It's not going to happen, because Israeli women and children need to go to sleep at night.* The film included protesters being told of Doron Spielman's concern to protect Israeli lives. Some replied that, if a protective wall was necessary, it should be built on Israeli territory, without stealing Palestinian villagers' land.

The stand-off continued over 55 protests. Both sides showed restraint. Doron Spielman said, *Thank God, as you can see, things are taking place, there's been no violence.* But in 2005 village boys threw stones at the soldiers, causing injuries. Some village men supported the boys, but the women tried to persuade them against violence. The soldiers responded with tear gas, stun grenades and bullets. Two comments each seem true. An Israeli activist said: *The strategy of the struggle is non-violence. That does not mean that, with enough provocation by the army, people won't throw stones.* And Doron Spielman said: *As an Israeli soldier, an 18-year-old boy has been trained in the Israeli army, a very well-run organized army, but at the end of the day he is a boy, and if he feels a rock swung over his head, then he's stressed.* Ayed Morrar said he wanted total non-violence. Captain Spielman said that, in carrying out his orders, he wanted to violate the villagers' rights as little as possible. Yasmine Levy appreciated the villagers' case. Cynics might dismiss what each said as public relations. Interpreting motives is obviously fallible. But, in the *Budrus* interviews, from all three I had a strong impression of seriousness and integrity.

Entrapment

Budrus was a microcosm of the wider conflict. With enough provocation by the army, some 'non-violent' young men will throw stones. If a rock is swung over the head of a teenage soldier, his stress may lead to violent retaliation. Accused of stealing Palestinian land and livelihood, Doron Spielman cited the need to keep civilians safe from terrorism. This 'debate' was not face-to-face, but separate interviews to camera. Had it been closer and more extended, Ayed Morrar could say that terrorism, while wrong, was a response to occupation. Doron Spielman could reply that occupation was a response to the 1967 attack on Israel. But Ayed Morrar might say … Some children enjoy what (perhaps mistakenly) they think an insoluble question: which came first – the chicken or the egg? The debate over the wall spirals out to 1967, to 1947–8, and beyond living memory to the nineteenth century. Those trapped in Budrus were trapped in history too.

Those leading on the ground in Budrus (Ayed Morrar, Doron Spielman and Yasmine Levy) were severely limited by policies made by their national leaders. Doron Spielman had no power to change the route of the wall. Palestinian leaders seemed only coolly supportive of the non-violent campaign. At Ayed Morrar's invitation, Palestine's Prime Minister, Salaam Fayyad, visited the protest. He appears, shaking hands and having a brief word, but – at least in the documentary – does not seem engaged. Morrar afterwards said his relationship with such officials was very touchy: *You know their importance, but they don't feel your importance or value. They think the whole world is a tent and they control the tent, and everyone must play by their rules.* The leaderships on both sides have everyone in a trap. They too are trapped. If Palestine Authority leaders repeatedly made statements strongly condemning all violence, many of those subject to checkpoint humiliations, night raids and house demolitions might switch support to Hamas. An Israeli government ending all repression might be accused of betrayal of Zionism. Two peoples, two leaderships, a four-way entrapment. I hope there are political scientists and game theorists working out escape strategies. Meanwhile some pessimism seems hard to avoid.

Not Victory but Transformation

Non-violence is sometimes seen as a gentler version of war: a contest in which one side will *peacefully* defeat the other. But Sari Nusseibeh cites Gandhi: *a key feature of Gandhi's power of the soul is transformation, not subjection. The guiding imperative here should not be winning over the other side, but winning the other side over.*[9]

Gandhi is right that it is better when it is language, saying we need not be enemies. Best of all is when the monologue moves to conversation, when the message sent is given a peaceful response. In Budrus there was communication across barriers between army and villagers. It is hard to know the previous attitudes of Doron Spielman or Yasmine Levy. He may have cared already about respecting Palestinian rights; she may have cared already about not destroying villagers' olive trees. But perhaps the (largely) non-violent confrontation made these concerns more vivid.

On the Palestinian side, too, there was communication across barriers: those excluding Hamas from the non-violence, and those about keeping women out of the protest. But there were also changes in how Israelis (and, more broadly, Jews) were seen by Palestinians including the Hamas member Ahmed Awwad: *I saw in reality Israelis defending me from the soldiers of the occupation. It was strange to see a Jew standing side by side with me, and our common enemy was a Jew as well, the soldier who is occupying my land. In these marches I saw these Israeli voices in real life. It wasn't just something I heard about.*

Like Ahmed Awwad, Iltezam Morrar started to have a more complex view of Israelis: *I don't know Israelis. I just know the soldiers. I went many times to my father in the prison and all the Israelis I met were very, very bad. But now I know that not all the Israelis are the same. Some of them think that we should live together in peace. I did not think that one day I would have Israeli friends or even talk to Israeli women. Not all of them are soldiers, they don't really hate us.*

Elsewhere sometimes, quite independent of Budrus, there are parallel Palestinian responses to some Israelis. Rabbi Arik Ascherman, of Rabbis for Human Rights, reported something Palestinian parents said: *We want you to meet our children. Our ten-year-old has just seen his home demolished in front of his eyes; he's just seen his parents humiliated in front of his eyes. What do we say to our ten-year-old child when he says, 'I want to grow up and be a terrorist'? We want him to know that not every Israeli comes with guns to demolish our homes; that there are Israelis that are willing to stand shoulder-to-shoulder with us to rebuild our homes.*[10]

III: Three Psychological Fault Lines Central to the Conversation: Backlash, Rigid Belief, Identity Traps

Amos Oz was right that friendly encounters across the barriers are nice, but nowhere near enough to make peace: *Rivers of coffee drunk together cannot extinguish the tragedy of two peoples claiming, and I think rightly claiming, the same small country as their one and only national homeland in the whole world. So drinking coffee is wonderful ... But drinking coffee cannot do away with the trouble. What we need is not just coffee and a better understanding. What we need is a painful compromise.*[11]

Clearly chat over coffee is not enough. A compromise *is* needed. But was Oz mistaken in implying 'a better understanding' was no more relevant to compromise than coffee drinking? There is such limited understanding of the conflict's psychology. Many round the world demand a decent respect to the opinions of mankind. The West-Eastern Divan orchestra is heartening. It is inspiring when David Shulman defends a beleaguered Al-Quds in the name of the core values of a university. Long may these things help break down barriers. But neither side seems ready to change 'tough' official policies. Fragments of the conversation of mankind are heard. But Israeli governments and Hamas defend their nation with violence: 'the only language the other side understand'.

The UNESCO Constitution says, *Since wars begin in the minds of men, it is in the minds of men that the defence of peace must be constructed.* This is only part of the truth. Causes of war are not all psychological. They include material things like land, oil and water. But a huge contribution to the Israel–Palestine conflict is made by three fault lines, whose deep psychology is central to the remaining half of this book. First: the heart of cycles of violence is the psychology of backlash. Second: rigid belief systems, religious or political, block the give and take of making peace. Third are links between conflict and identity. The passions of long enmity between peoples can harden the hostility into an aggressive identity of their own.

Political leaders may not know relevant studies by historians, psychologists, psychotherapists, anthropologists, philosophers and others. Little understanding of these fault lines has entered public consciousness. But to end the cycle of violence, they and their harm must be understood. This book is being completed at one of the conflict's darker times, but there is reason for modest long-term hope. Good education includes the chance better to understand ourselves and our world. These parts of our psychology, and critical thinking about them, deserve a place. If children and young adults get used to discussing them, conversations – even over coffee – may start to make a difference.

PART TWO
BACKLASH

How shall we sing the Lord's song in a strange land? ... O daughter of Babylon, who art to be destroyed: happy shall he be, that destroyeth thee as thou hast served us. Happy shall he be, that taketh and dasheth thy little ones against the stones.
PSALM 137, verses 8 and 9.

To be revenged was in more request than never to have received injury.
THUCYDIDES: *The Peloponnesian War*, translated by Thomas Hobbes, Book 3, 82.

Beowulf, son of Ecgtheow, spoke:
'Wise sir, do not grieve. It is always better
to avenge dear ones than to indulge in mourning.'
BEOWULF, translated by Seamus Heaney.

My life hatred has been for Germany because of what she has done to France.
GEORGES CLEMENCEAU, prime supporter at Versailles of the harsh peace terms for Germany, quoted in Margaret Macmillan: *Paris 1919, Six Months that Changed the World.*

William Shirer described Hitler's expression on the day of his 1940 triumph at Compiègne: a sort of scornful, inner joy at being present at this great reversal of fate ... he himself had wrought ..., as his eyes meet ours, you grasp the depth of his

*hatred. But there is triumph there too – revengeful, trium-
phant hate ... He swiftly snaps his hands on his hips, arches
his shoulders, plants his feet wide apart ... a magnificent
gesture of burning contempt for this place and all that it
has stood for since it witnessed the humbling of the German
Empire*
WILLIAM SHIRER: *Berlin Diary, 1934–1941.*

*If tonight the people of London were asked to cast their
votes whether a convention should be entered into to stop the
bombing of all cities, the overwhelming majority would cry,
'No, we will mete out to the Germans the measure, and more
than the measure, that they have meted out to us'.*
WINSTON CHURCHILL, to cheers in London, July 1941.

*Those who maintain that this war is against terrorism, what
is this terrorism that they talk about at a time when people
of the umma have been slaughtered for decades..? When the
victim starts to avenge the innocent children in Palestine,
Iraq, southern Sudan, Somalia, Kashmir, and the Philippines,
the hypocrites and ruler's jurists stand up and defend this
blatant unbelief – I seek God's help against them all.*
OSAMA BIN LADEN, soon after 9/11, on the war in
Afghanistan.

*I can hear you. The rest of the world hears you. And the
people who knocked these buildings down will hear all of us
soon.*
PRESIDENT GEORGE W. BUSH, in the ruins of the World
Trade Center, before launching the Iraq war.

5
THE PSYCHOLOGY OF BACKLASH

Backlash's grip on human psychology is illustrated by the thoughts just cited from different cultures at different times. It seems plausible that it had an evolutionary origin. If one creature reacted to attacks with backlash while the other responded peacefully, it seems unlikely that pacifism would triumph in the Darwinian struggle.

I: The Blood-Feud Version

A blood-feud arises only when a person kills, harms or humiliates someone in another group. Backlash is central. Those on both sides may think revenge justified. The feuds are *inside* nations, sometimes between different tribes, sometimes between clans or families in the same tribe. Anthropologists and historians rightly distinguish them from the official standing and huge scope of national wars.

Here, studies of four blood-feuds (a small fraction of those known) will be drawn on. The Franks were a Germanic people from east of the Rhine, who conquered what is now France. Their period, around 450–750 CE, was one of blood-feud. So was the period of the thirteenth century Icelandic sagas. And so, one and a half millennia after that, were the

1930s among the Nuer in the Sudan. So too the tribesmen of
Montenegro in the 1960s.

Feuds' psychological grip was strong, usually overcoming
any religious opposition. Christianity, deeply rooted
in medieval Iceland, did not ban 'justifiable' vengeance.
Centuries earlier, the Franks' Christianity condemned blood-
feuding, but could not stop it. *Hot blood was never to be
overlooked; while in it, a man and his kin might be excused
almost anything, and no amount of teaching ever persuaded
the medieval mind that it was wrong.*[1]

Medieval Iceland: The Cloak

*Hildegunn came into the room and went up to Flosi, pushed her
hair back from her eyes, and wept. Flosi said, 'You are sad now,
kinswoman, you are weeping. It is only right that you should
weep over a good husband'. 'What redress will you get me?' she
asked. 'How much help will you give me?' 'I shall press your
claims to the full extent of the law', said Flosi, 'or else conclude
a settlement ... which will satisfy all the demands of honour'.*

*Hildegunn said, 'Hoskuld would have avenged you with
blood ... Arnor Ornolfsson never did your father as grave an
injury as this and yet your brothers Kolbein and Egil killed
him'. She walked from the room and unlocked her chest.
She took out the cloak, the gift from Flosi, which Hoskuld
had been wearing when he was killed and in which she had
preserved all his blood. Flosi had finished eating ... She then
threw the cloak around his shoulders and the clotted blood
rained down all over him ...*

*'This is the cloak you gave to Hoskuld ... He was wearing
it when he was killed. I call upon God and all good men to
witness that I charge you in the name of all the powers of
your Christ and in the name of all your courage and your
manhood, to avenge every one of the wounds that marked his
body – or be an object of contempt to all men.'*
NJAL'S SAGA, Iceland, about 1280, translated by Magnus
Magnusson and Hermann Palsson

Feuds had rules about both vengeance and compensation.
They had to fit the offence. What was the tariff? Icelanders
used the *metaphor of symmetry and balanced exchange*,
in which *corpse was set against corpse, injury balanced
against insult, and what was left over was weighed against*

compensation in property.[2] But there was inevitable arbitrariness in this 'balancing'.

The Franks had no other redress: *without the sanction of blood, composition* [compensation] *would have stood a poor chance in a world lacking not simply a police force but the requisite concept of public order.*[3] In the 1930s, E.E. Evans-Pritchard saw backlash as protecting the Nuer: *When a man feels that he has suffered an injury there is no authority ... from whom he can obtain redress, so he at once challenges the man who has wronged him to a duel ... a man's courage is his only immediate protection against aggression.*[4] It was the same in Montenegro. There was no authority to arrange redress. To preserve their honour people had to take the law into their own hands: *there exists no centralized political power to step in and control homicidal conflicts within the group.*[5] In Scotland in 1593, this led to dramatic protests: *some poor women from Nithsdale travelled up to Edinburgh with the bloody shirts of their husbands, sons and servants who had been slain in a raid by the Johnstones. Carrying these gory objects, they paraded through the burgh exposing the king's inadequacy in providing protection or justice.*[6]

Weakening the Grip of 'Justified Backlash'?

Sometimes a blood-feud episode could be *ended* through compromise. Among the Nuer, agreement could be negotiated by one of the respected 'Leopard-skin chiefs'.[7] In Montenegro a Court of Good Men could help if both sides wanted an agreement.[8] But no authority could impose a solution *before* a blood-feud began. A feud could not be prevented by ruling a victim had been wronged. This is one link with the Israel–Palestine conflict. In current disputes between nations there is a 'preventive' gap, one the UN lacks power to fill with adjudications backed by sanctions.

Bitterness may remain even after settling a violent feud. Among the Nuer, *close kinsmen on either side will not eat with one another for years, even for a generation or two ... 'A bone (the dead man) lies between them' ... all Nuer recognize that in spite of payments and sacrifices a feud goes on for ever, for the dead man's kin never cease 'to have war in their hearts' ... the sore rankles and the feud, though formally concluded, may at any time break out again.*[9] This was reflected in scepticism about feud-settling among the Franks: *feuds are like volcanoes. A few are in eruption, others are extinct, but most are content to rumble now and again and leave us guessing.*[10] Blood-feuds (hard to prevent, hard to bring to a decisive end) flourished across the world and across millennia. They shared a persistent pattern, centred on believing backlash justified.

II: Wounds – Dignity and Humiliation

Typically, backlash is a reaction to killing or to insults to dignity. But sometimes dignity can be the response to insult. Mahmoud Darwish's grandfather refused to sell the Israelis his land: *After it was confiscated, the land became a source of misery as well as the foundation of personal and national dignity. Having opted for dignity, he died within sight of the crime and his torture: 'I will not sell them my land even if I die of hunger'.*[11] Stubbornness asserted moral status. He, like his land, could not be bought. His grandson linked this with dignity: the claim to be treated with respect.

Avishai Margalit's *The Decent Society* at the start makes dignity central: *A decent society is one whose institutions do not humiliate people.*[12] Michael Rosen makes dignity not just about actions, but also about attitudes we communicate. *We may (under certain circumstances) fight our enemies, but we may not humiliate them; we may punish criminals, but we must not degrade them.*[13] It excludes Yasser Arafat's order to security forces to humiliate Hamas supporters by shaving their beards. One former head of Shin Bet denied that policy had reduced terrorism. If we believe every person has dignity to be respected, this means not humiliating anyone.

Interrogation with Psychological Pressure

Sari Nusseibeh, the distinguished philosopher and President of Al-Quds University, supported the First Intifada. He opposes violence, but it included violent acts. Shin Bet had a case to interrogate him as one of the leaders. 'We may (under certain circumstances) interrogate our enemies, but we may not humiliate them.' After hours of questioning, the approach changed to laughing and joking. *The inflection in their voices was now vulgar* ... *'Your wife is English, isn't she?' ('English' was repeated between them a number of times, each time with snickers.) What's her name? It's Lucy, right? Luuucy. (More giggling.) 'She drives around in a red Peugeot, doesn't she?' one crowed. 'Yeah, with yellow plates', another chipped in* ... *'Aren't you worried that some people might think she's an Israeli?... Your own intifada guys could easily mistake her for the enemy, (Ha-ha-ha-ha!) She could end up inside her car from those Molotov cocktails your leaflets are so full of.' One officer at this point wagged his head in mock commiseration with me. 'Poor Luuucy.'*[14] Then came more 'amusing' disrespect and 'joking' threats against his children and his mother. It was the cold joke again. (Last heard here in the 'amusing' thought of Dov Weisglass that the Israeli blockade causing food shortages in Gaza was 'putting the Palestinians on a diet'.) Victims are meant to find the cold joke humiliating, but certainly not funny. Its message: we have the power to do terrible things to you or to people you care about. We don't care about your humiliation or distress so we treat it as amusing. Just hearing the joke humiliates the victim. These cases – Arafat and beards, the interrogation of Nusseibeh, putting Palestinians on a diet – express some of the most disgusting attitudes Michael Rosen wants ruled out.

6

THE ILLUSIONS OF
BACKLASH

Although deep in our psychology, backlash can be weakened. After terrible wounds, some people reject backlash, hoping to understand and to avoid repetition. A week after her brother went missing in the World Trade Center on 9/11, Catherine Dawson wrote a letter: *When atrocities have happened to other people and they have reacted with hatred, wanting immediate revenge ... I've always said that it's impossible to know how one would react in such a situation. You can't blame others when you don't know how they feel. My brother is missing and it's hard to stay optimistic. But I don't want to rush and attack the people who have done this. I want to understand how it could happen. I want someone to make sure that it never happened again so that other people don't have to experience what our family is going through. Bombing other people will not stop that happening again ... How have we managed to get our world in such a mess?*[1]

Not everyone has such understanding or such lack of vengefulness. Deep psychological fault lines cannot be legislated away. But one hope of gradually weakening backlash's appeal may come from questioning some of its illusions.

I: 'Teach Them a Lesson': Illusions of Deterrence

At the village of Isawiyya, David Shulman wondered about humiliation and embitterment. *The other roads in and out of the village are still functional; so why have they put up this ugly barrier ... right here on the one road that would make life a bit easier for these people? Unless, of course, the whole point is simply to humiliate and embitter them, to show them who is master.*[2]

Humiliation at checkpoints has been defended as disrupting terrorism. Scott Atran described one incident to a friend, who raised it with the then Prime Minister. Arial Sharon responded: *Don't you understand? I want them to feel humiliated, and we'll keep doing it until they stop trying to kill us.* He assumed a deterrence that justifies over-riding decent behaviour and the attitudes it expresses. He left out the cycle of violence. Scott Atran remembered humiliated Palestinians: *the angry eyes of the old lady, her boys and the crowd showed me they were far from cowed.*[3]

Dr Abdul Rantisi, defending Hamas suicide bombings, said they started targeting Israeli civilians only in response to Israeli atrocities like Dr Baruch Goldstein's Ramadan massacre in Hebron: *if we did not respond in this way, Israelis would keep doing the same thing. Moreover, the bombings were a moral lesson. They were a way of making innocent Israelis feel the pain Palestinians had felt.* Perhaps his reaction to the Israeli killing of some of his family blinded him to a question his own history suggested. Is killing people on the other side an intelligent way to teach anyone a moral lesson? The implied claim about Israeli psychology is so crude: horrible retaliation deters them from further action. Standing against that is the whole history of cycles of violence. The wildly wrong claim raises doubts about Rantisi's self-knowledge. Perhaps, after his own tragic history at Israeli hands, he wanted revenge but disguised it to himself as a moral lesson?

II: Magical Metaphysics

Sometimes things nearly all of us believe and occasionally act on, when clearly and simply stated, are seen to be obviously false. Martha Nussbaum did this to believers in the central assumption of backlash. *They should not suppose that proportional suffering rights wrongs. This archaic and powerful thought grips most of us; but it is a form of magical metaphysics that does not stand the light of reason ... Murder is not undone by any amount of suffering on the part of the perpetrator, nor is any other crime.*[4]

The central illusion is that murder is somehow undone by retaliation. *Literal* believers in the magical metaphysics, that killing her killer brings your daughter back, are non-existent. However, the magic may sometimes have left a kind of shadow, influencing responses despite not being believed.

People have less fantastic real hopes whose satisfaction is still important. The best outcome is the perpetrator's seeing and regretting the harm done, accepting responsibility for it and apologizing. Understanding there is no better outcome could be helped by the handling in class (or in families) of children's quarrels, fights or bullying. It is why, to end cycles of violence between peoples, Truth and Reconciliation Commissions do matter.

III: The Mirage of 'Getting Even'

No doubt there are various causes of different kinds of suicide attacks. A perceptive diagnosis of one possible cause of Palestinian suicide bombing comes from Alice Chalvi, who taught English Literature at the Hebrew University of Jerusalem: *Palestinian despair is now so deep that there is a kind of comfort to kill the other side – to do unto us as we have done to them. It's that sense of pride that is so terrible. The Palestinian people must be in such a state of despair to kill themselves or to glory in the deaths of their children.*[5]

Ami Ayalon's insight came in conversation with Dr Eyad Sarraj, who said, *Ami, we finally beat you.* They both knew hundreds of Palestinians had been killed in the intifada, and a Palestinian state was probably lost. Ayalon asked, *that's victory?* Sarraj replied, *you don't understand us. Victory for us is to see you suffer. That's all we want ... Finally, after fifty years, we've achieved a balance of power, a parity. Your F16 opposite our suicide bomber.*[6]

'Getting even' could make conflict endless. Usually there is no way to show things are now 'even'. William Ian Miller makes this point about blood-feuds in medieval Iceland: *Favouring interminability was the fact that few return blows ever precisely balanced the wrong they were matched against. The notion of balance itself was innately ambiguous since it was not mathematical, but socially contingent on a host of shifting variables, some of which were subject to conscious manipulation by the parties.*[7] Unsurprisingly, this problem for medieval Icelanders has left modern avengers with the same incoherent aim. They never feel 'enough is enough'.

IV: The Illusion of Collective Guilt

Even if backlash did reduce the other group's violence, who would we be punishing? Abdul Rantisi's hope of teaching a 'moral lesson' reflects the central assumption: collective guilt. People project on to 'enemy' groups a uniform identity. 'They' are all guilty and deserve what they get. Even babies and young children? Stated clearly, this is obviously an illusion. But it traps people on both sides in a cycle they do not understand.

After 9/11 Osama bin Laden celebrated victory over a stereotyped America. He said they had rubbed America's nose in the dirt. Around 3,000 people were killed. Did they *all* support American policies in the Muslim world? Should the American Muslims killed have had their noses rubbed in the dirt? What about the people killed from Colombia, Japan, Jamaica, Mexico and the Philippines? Collective guilt rests on the stereotype. It depends on avoiding questions about actual people killed.

President Bush, starting the 'war on terror', promised the perpetrators of 9/11 'will hear from us all soon'. But how many of more than 3,000 Afghan civilians killed were involved in 9/11? Were there really more people in the conspiracy than were killed by it? What of the perhaps 600,000 killed in the Iraq war? Possibly none were involved. American public support for the war was linked to hitting back at Iraq's supposed Al-Qaeda terrorism. Behind this was the illusion of collective guilt.

7
COLLECTIVE GUILT: THE ROLE OF STEREOTYPES

Belief in collective guilt was heard in the words of Mohammad Sidique Khan, one of the bombers who struck in London in 2005. His chosen identity was Muslim. The British were 'you': *Our words have no impact on you, therefore I'm going to talk to you in a language you understand. Our words are dead until we give them life with our blood ... Your democratically elected governments continuously perpetrate atrocities against my people all over the world. And your support of them makes you directly responsible ... Until we feel security, you will be our targets. And until you stop the bombing, gassing, imprisonment and torture of my people we will not stop this fight. We are at war and I am a soldier. Now you too will taste the reality of this situation.*[1]

The illusion needs the stereotype. 'You' are all impervious to what Muslims say, so 'blood' is 'a language you understand'. 'Your' support of governments committing atrocities against Muslims 'makes you directly responsible'. Mohammad Sidique Khan's bomb at Edgware Road station killed six other people. He did not ask if some might be British *and* Muslim. (The Edgware Road has many Middle Eastern shops and restaurants.) And how could he know that the six people killed were among the minority who supported the Iraq war? The political demonstration against it was at that time London's largest ever. Did the demonstrators deserve to be killed? Stereotypes of collective guilt do not survive such questions. Hope might come from understanding of how the stereotypes are created and maintained.

I: Rival Narratives: Lebanon, 2006

Hostile group stereotypes are often supported by rival stories of their shared history. Many Israelis disagree with each other. So do many Palestinians. But there is on each side a widely supported official narrative of the conflict. Take the narratives of one episode between Israel and Lebanon. In 2006, Ali Fayyad, of the Hizbullah Executive Committee, and Isaac Herzog, a minister in the Israeli Security Cabinet, gave their views to the *Guardian*.[2]

Ali Fayyad's general view was: *For nearly two weeks Israel has been waging a war of terror and aggression against Lebanon ... The war has already resulted in the killing of around 400 and wounding of more than 1,000 Lebanese. Most are civilians (a third children), crushed in their homes or ripped to pieces in their cars by Israeli bombs and missiles.*

Isaac Herzog's general view was: *Israel today is facing a sustained onslaught from one of the world's most dangerous and effective terrorist organizations. In the past few days, 1,000 rockets and 1,200 mortar rounds have been hurled across the border by Hizbullah at hospitals, schools and homes ... Israel is fighting back. Israel's use of force is entirely proportionate to the extent of the threat that Hizbullah poses. A third of our people are in immediate danger of Hizbullah missiles and are sheltering for fear of their lives.*

They also disagreed over who started it.

Isaac Herzog: *Israel was forced to enter this conflict after an unprovoked attack by Hizbullah terrorists across the border, in which three soldiers were killed and two kidnapped.*

Ali Fayyad: *In the context of the continued occupation, detention of prisoners and incursions into Lebanese territory, the capture of the Israeli soldiers was entirely legitimate. The operation was fully in line with ... the right of the resistance to liberate occupied Lebanese territory, free prisoners of war and defend Lebanon against Israeli aggression.*

They disagreed over the two sides' intentions.

Isaac Herzog: *Their intention is the killing and maiming of Israelis in general.*

Ali Fayyad: *Hizbullah has tried from the start ... to limit the escalation by adopting a policy of limited response while avoiding civilian targets.*

Isaac Herzog: *Israel's goal, first and foremost, is to ensure that, when our operations end, Hizbullah no longer controls the border with Israel, and may not reignite fighting at its whim.*

Ali Fayyad: *The Israeli onslaught is aimed not only at liquidating the resistance and destroying the country's infrastructure but at intervening in Lebanese politics and imposing conditions on what can be agreed.*

Each sees their side's actions as legitimate defence against the other's aggression:

Ali Fayyad: *International law also allows peoples and states to take action to protect their citizens and territory.*

Isaac Herzog: *International law recognizes the right to respond to the extent of a threat and Israel has therefore acted within international law.*

II: Narratives and Stereotypes in Mutual Support

Each side's narrative of the whole conflict interacts with interpretations of particular episodes. Why does Isaac Herzog think Hizbullah intends to kill and maim Israelis? Why not accept Ali Fayyad's account that they have tried to avoid civilian targets? Why does Ali Fayyad think Israel intends to liquidate resistance, destroy the infrastructure, intervene in Lebanese politics and impose conditions on agreement? Why not accept Isaac Herzog's account that the intention is to prevent Hizbullah controlling the border and re-starting the fighting? Their replies can be imagined. Each would see the hostile account of the other as far more plausible. 'You can't believe Hizbullah: they have a record of attacks on civilians'. 'You can't believe Israeli is only defensive: their record is one of domination and expansion'. In these self-perpetuating narratives, the stereotype weights interpretation of every

episode; each episode reinforces the stereotype. And where
a stereotype is unconscious, dislodging it may be nearly
impossible.

III: Unconscious Seeing and Stereotyping

A woman Israeli citizen aged about twenty, the daughter of
an Arab father and a Jewish mother, saw things in a more
complex way than many did: *Sometimes I am the only one
among my Jewish and Arab friends who can see how much
the preconceptions of both sides are similar, how each side
uses exactly the same kinds of preconceptions and stereotypes with regard to the other.*[3]

More goes on in seeing and thinking than most of us
know. About acquiring knowledge, Kant saw the limits of
simple empiricism. Our minds don't passively accept the
world's imprint. We impose our categories and concepts on
our experience. Kant's revolution now has huge scientific
support. Neuroscientists map complex mechanisms of visual
interpretation from the retina to the visual cortex. It is not
just that a 'picture' emerges and the person then interprets
it as a face. The experienced 'picture' itself depends on
unconscious processes. These are rule-governed layers of
programmed interpretation: *the pattern of activity on the
cortex is anything but a reproduction of the outside scene. If
it were, that would mean only that nothing interesting had
happened between eye and cortex.*[4]

This applies even to apparently simple questions. 'What
colour is this flower?' The colour you see depends on
surrounding context. David Marr put it intuitively: *Suppose
you pass an embankment where a yellow or blue flower
happens to be growing amid a background of green grass
and clover ... If the flower appears lighter than the grass,
this is probably due to a characteristic of the flower and not
of the illumination.*[5] To construct the colour of a surface,
the brain compares the ratio of light of any given waveband
to light of the same waveband reflected from the surround.
This is then compared with other information about shape,
etc. As Semir Zeki puts it, colour is *a comparison of
comparisons.*[6]

Donald Hoffman outlines both the complexity and the brain's response. *As always, the images are infinitely ambiguous ... There are countless ways in which you could interpret an image in terms of objects, their shape, their colours and their illuminants ... But again, you have rules ... by which you select one interpretation from the countless possibilities.*[7] Hoffman gives rules for interpreting *changes* in hue, saturation and brightness. Interpret *gradual* changes as changes in *illumination* but interpret *abrupt* changes as changes in *surfaces*. We do not notice these rules operating. The brain follows them on automatic pilot.

One way of thinking of rules of interpretation is as 'perceptual hypotheses'. Richard Gregory, coining that phrase, thought the brain *is like a scientist looking for regularities upon which to base predictions*. He saw perception as *a continually changing hypothesis of the world, which is tested by sensory data and stored generalizations based on past experience ... perception of an object is similar to a hypothesis in science.*[8] The parallel with scientists changing hypotheses as new evidence is discovered is a good one. It fits interpretation far beyond recognizing colours.

Scientists are not alone in knowing the role of prior hypotheses in the mind's activity. On this, the great twentieth-century humanist was Ernst Gombrich, claiming (against the impressionists) that there is no such thing as the innocent eye. His many illustrations suggest representational artists see what they paint through stereotypes, often from earlier art. They use 'schema and correction'. *You must have a starting point, a standard of comparison, in order to begin that process of making and matching which finally becomes embodied in the finished image. The artist cannot start from scratch but he can criticize his forerunners.*[9]

These voices from philosophy, neuroscience and art history suggest some stereotypes may be too rooted to eliminate. What might this mean for tribal conflict? We do not yet know how extensive is the brain's unconscious use of embedded categories. Embedded rules harmlessly steer us to see red or green. But some potential uses could seem more like hostile stereotyping than science. Unconscious rules drawn from conflict narratives could steer us to see people as enemies: terrorists or cruel occupiers, anti-Semites or infidels. Depending on how the evidence turns out, future neuroscience of stereotypes could discover deep difficulties.[10]

IV: Against Stereotypes: The Duck-Rabbit

Joseph Jastrow, noticing the ambiguous 'duck-rabbit' figure in a magazine, argued that seeing depends on the eye that sees. Ludwig Wittgenstein famously discussed the duck-rabbit, wondering what happens in our minds when seeing a duck changes to seeing a rabbit. The 'tribal narratives' interest here is closer to Jastrow's striking phrase: *the realm where fancy soars free from the confines of sense.*[11]

Figure 5: The Duck-Rabbit

They say the land is theirs, but we were here first and they took it from us.
But, even before that, we were here. It was ours and we were driven away first.
The British promised that we could have our state here.
But they said the same to us too.
It was the Nakba.
It was the War of Independence.
It was a duck.
It was a rabbit.
It is Palestine.

It is Israel.
It is a duck.
It is a rabbit.
Hermann von Helmholtz said perception involves 'unconscious conclusions', which, because unconscious, are irresistible.[12] Even knowing the duck-rabbit is ambiguous, we do not see both at once, but oscillate between the two. Despite our critical powers, the subjective feel persists. We cannot eliminate stereotypes from our thinking. But, aware, we can weaken their influence. Gombrich's phrase is a good one: schema *and correction.* Perhaps sometimes we must *start* from a stereotype, but a critical attitude can seep in. Getting to know someone can help escape the group stereotype. People knowing about ambiguous figures still cannot see duck and rabbit simultaneously, but can avoid futile arguments about which it really is. Rising above rival stereotypes is not easy. Nor is it impossible.

V: Looking Through the Stereotypes

Members of some professions, perhaps through a combination of their training and their own humanity, find their work leads to looking through the stereotype to the person behind it. It is striking how often this is true of medical professionals. In her book on suicide bombing, Barbara Victor brings out some medical responses to victims. Here are three:

> Gimella, a nurse from a small Palestinian village near Jerusalem, says, 'I leave my politics at the door … All I see are people in terrible need of my expertise and care, and I administer it without any hesitation. My goal is to save lives. My patients have no nationality or religion.' The Israeli doctor nods. 'I have a Palestinian man in this bed who has a fierce infection from his injuries, and I have an Israeli man in the bed next to him who lost a leg and risks losing the other leg from a suicide bombing. I don't care how each of them got here … I care that they will leave here alive.'[13]
>   A Palestinian nurse treating Israeli victims felt it was *just unbearable to see these two people so broken, so grief-stricken. One moment they were all on their way, as a*

*family, to a joyous event, and the next minute they are in
mourning.*

   She spent hours with them, and settled them in adjoining
beds. But the man *asked me if I was an Arab. I answered that
I was a Palestinian. They both began to hit me and pull my
hair ... I don't blame them. How would I feel in their position
if an Israeli was tending to me and telling me that an Israeli
had just killed my children? ... I grieve for all the parents who
lose children and for all the children who lose parents. There
is no easy answer.*[14]

VI: Dialogue and Reconciliation

People may never agree about previous wars. In peace-making
should we ignore the rival narratives? 'Forget the past. How can
we live together in peace from now on?' But the unhistorical
approach leaves out the need for recognition and apology for
atrocities. With so much bitterness, how can the history be
confronted? After apartheid, the Truth and Reconciliation
Commission looked back for things to learn. Only then was
learning possible. Many would not have testified earlier.
But needs the Commission met had been present during the
conflict. Its work may help Israeli–Palestinian peace-making.
What sort of truth? How does it relate to reconciliation?

   One target was both sides' false claims. The African
National Congress had carried out atrocities: 'necklacing'
Black South Africans thought disloyal to the cause, murdering
White farmers. Apartheid's defenders (not just 'a few rotten
apples') tortured and killed opponents. Both sides had denied
much. The Commission cited Yugoslavia, stressing danger in
selective versions of history.[15]

   The Commission wanted more than who did what to
whom? They sought deeper truths about what these acts
meant to victims and perpetrators. Victims telling their own
stories might yield 'narrative truth', validating experiences
of people previously silenced or voiceless. The Commission
also wanted 'dialogue truth', through discussion and debate.
There was 'healing truth', seeing what facts mean in human
relationships, and public recognition that they had been
wronged. *The public victim hearings vividly portrayed the*

fact that ... not only was there a disrespect for human rights in the abstract, but the very dignity and 'personhood' of individual human beings were violated.

The Commission knew wanting revenge is natural. Suppressing anger undermines reconciliation. They wanted not retribution but a justice reconciling victims and perpetrators. Victims would not forgive if that meant forgetting. Trying not to be bitter is not forgetting. They wanted their story fully heard and accepted: *an affirmation that the person's pain is real and worthy of attention. It is thus central to the restoration of the dignity of victims.*[16]

No Commission is likely during the Israel–Palestine conflict. But informal dialogue with a historical dimension is possible. The South African model could help human responses break through stereotypes and denial. Settling for understanding short of agreement would help. Both sides might accept that different views exist. Sometimes avoiding the past may be necessary. But it may be worth going as deep as the conversation will bear, exploring what wounds mean to people and their need for recognition of this.

Remembering the conflict, as in the Truth and Reconciliation Commission, is important. But some 'forgetfulness' can be creative. Not amnesia, but a shared agreement to leave the past behind. In 1648, those making the Peace of Westphalia to end the Thirty Years' War knew that dwelling on suffering and humiliation can breed violence. The peace treaties were explicit: *Both sides grant the other a perpetual oblivion and amnesty for all that ... has been done to the other since the beginning of these troubles, so that neither for any of these things, nor upon any other account or pretext whatsoever, any act of hostility, enmity, vexation or hindrance shall be exercised ... Instead, each and every injury, act of violence, hostility, damage and expense inflicted by either side, both before and during the war, by words, in writing or by deed, shall be entirely forgotten.*[17] 'Entirely forgotten' was probably not meant literally. Not understood at Versailles at the end of the First World War, but recognized by de Gaulle and Adenauer at the end of the Second, was the need to grant oblivion for past wrongs.

Four hundred and fifty years after Westphalia, the 1998 Northern Ireland Peace Agreement had the same aim: *We must never forget those who have died or been injured, and their families. But we can best honour them through a fresh start, in which we firmly dedicate ourselves to the achievement of reconciliation.*[18]

Figure 6: Josefina Vasconcellos: Reconciliation. 'Unfortunately plans for another sculpture to go in Jerusalem may have to wait for some time.'

PART THREE
RIGID BELIEFS AND IDENTITY

8

THE ROLE OF RIGID
BELIEFS

Figure 7: Drawing by Saul Steinberg

Saul Steinberg. Untitled, 1957. Ink on paper. Originally published in *The New Yorker*, June 1, 1957 © The Saul Steinberg Foundation/Artists Rights Society (ARS), NY/DACS, London 2023

> *All the stubborn arguers you meet are of the same brood. They never begin upon a subject they have not preresolved on. They want to hammer their nail into you and if you turn the point, still they think you wrong.*
> JOHN KEATS: Letter to George and Georgiana Keats, 17–27 September 1819.

I: 'Holy Land': Religious Blocks to Peace

My own morality doesn't matter. It is determined solely according to the Torah itself. The Torah is the brain. If the Torah tells you to do something that runs counter to your emotions, you do what runs counter to your emotions.
YIGAL AMIR, after killing Yitzhak Rabin, quoted in Dan Ephron: *Killing a King.*

The Prophet, prayer and peace be upon him, said: 'The time will not come until Muslims will fight the Jews (and kill them); until the Jews hide behind rocks and trees, which will cry: O Muslim! There is a Jew hiding behind me, come on and kill him!'
THE CHARTER OF HAMAS, article 7.[1]

Lord, what fools these mortals be!
PUCK, in A Midsummer Night's Dream.

Muslim obstacles to peace include the Quran's claims about iniquities of the Jews. There are Allah's supposed commands not to trust Jews as friends or allies. There is the role of Jerusalem in the story of the Prophet. On the side of Judaism, some believe God promised all the disputed land to Jews. Of course, many Palestinians and Israelis have versions of religion allowing them to doubt all that. But claims about God's promises or anger are still a real obstacle.

The Quran's references to Jews (and Christians) show awareness of the three religions as branches of the same tree. But some passages can fortify antisemitism, even when followed by qualifications. *God received a pledge from the Children of Israel ... God said, 'I am with you; if you perform the prayer, and pay the alms, and believe in My messengers and support them, and lend God a loan of righteousness, I will remit your sins, and admit you into Gardens beneath which rivers flow. But whoever among you disbelieves afterwards – he has strayed from the right way. Because of their breaking their pledge, We cursed them, and made their hearts hard. They twist the words out of their context, and they disregarded some of what they were reminded of. You will always witness deceit from them.*[2]

(This is followed by *But pardon them and overlook. God loves the doers of good.*) ... *And Due to wrongdoing on the part of the Jews, We forbade them good things that used to be lawful for them; and for deterring many from God's path. And for their taking usury, although they were forbidden it, and for their consuming people's wealth dishonestly. We have for the faithless among them a painful torment.*[3] (This is followed by praising Noah and the Prophets, and promising 'immense reward' to Jewish believers who pray and give to charity.)

In a 2014–15 opinion poll, 61 per cent of Israeli Jews said they believe Israel was given by God to the Jewish people. Genesis says God promised Abraham's descendants the land from the Nile to the Euphrates: *The LORD made a covenant with Abram, saying, Unto thy seed have I given this land, from the river of Egypt unto the great river, the river Euphrates.*[4] Muslims, too, claim descent from Ibrahim, though less is made of this in Islam. The supposed promise has many problems. From the Nile to the Euphrates is a lot of the Middle East. The Euphrates rises in Turkey, flows through Syria and Iraq, reaching the Persian Gulf on the Iraq–Iran frontier. Implementing God's promise would mean claiming a small bit of Turkey, a large part of Egypt including the Suez Canal, all of Jordan, all of Lebanon, a large slice of Saudi Arabia, around half of Iraq and two thirds of Syria. Even those who believe in God's promise might wonder about acting on it now.

The promise helped defeat the Oslo Agreement. To stop Oslo, Yigal Amir killed Rabin. The settler Hanan Porat condemned both the murder and Rabin: *A person who lifts his hand to uproot Jewish settlements from their land ... is not raising his hand against Hanan Porat ... he is raising his hand against the word of God that ordains 'that thy children shall come again to their own border'. Rabbi Nachum Rabinowitz said Rabin 'owed his life' for intending to hand over a Jew to non-Jewish authorities.*[5] Fanatics are a danger, and not only to those on the other side.

Jerusalem: The Noble Sanctuary and the Temple Mount

If I forget thee, O Jerusalem, let my right hand forget her cunning. If I do not remember thee, let my tongue cleave to

*the roof of my mouth, if I prefer not Jerusalem above my
chief joy.*
PSALM 137.

*The Mount is holy because of its history – which for some
believers stretches back to creation. Even more important is
its 'future history' ... the place where the drama of the End of
Days will come to pass. For Jewish extremists, Israel's failure
to take full possession of the Mount is an affront, for Islamic
extremists, Jewish rule is a desecration and an unending
threat.*
GERSHOM GORENBERG: *The End of Days.*

*Jews and Muslims, acting on religious beliefs and backed
up by nuclear capabilities, are poised to engage in history's
worst-ever massacre of human beings, over a rock.*
SARI NUSSEIBEH: *What is a Palestinian State Worth?*

Jerusalem is sacred to Muslims. They believe Allah led the
Prophet from Mecca to the al-Aqsa Mosque and then to
heaven. Many Jews think demolishing the al-Aqsa Mosque will
let their new Temple replace the one the Romans destroyed.
The issue is not helped by some American Christians: '*I think
there is a war coming within a year or two*' ... *smiling and
citing Ezekiel 38. It's a reference to the invasion of Israel by
the mythic forces of Magog, leading to the Last World War.
'Then the way will be paved for the Temple. We're reaching
the End of the Age'.*[6]

Public Policy: Bracketing off Claims Exclusive to Any One Religion

In Israel's Declaration of Independence, there is a promise
to *ensure complete equality of social and political rights
to all its inhabitants irrespective of religion, race or sex. It
will guarantee freedom of religion, conscience, language,
education and culture; it will safeguard the Holy Places of
all religions.*

This would be helped by Israelis bracketing off religious
belief from public policy. Laws applying to all should not
reflect commands accepted only by believers. Policy towards
other states should not be based on Divine Promises or Jihad.

Rigid beliefs make it very unlikely that either side would accept this bracketing off. In 1995, Binyamin Netanyahu promised that, if elected, he would arrange Jewish worship on the Mount, a promise it is a relief he did not keep. And he once presented a Christian Archbishop with a silver relief of Jerusalem with the Muslim shrines *replaced* by a Temple. Had he read the Declaration of Independence?

Peace-making depends on sympathetic but critical responses to rigid belief. More promising than questioning the existence of God is questioning different religion's claims about God's commands. Are there good reasons for choosing one version over others? Problems answering this may make different tribes of believers more tolerant of each other's foibles. (Religious counselling a bit like marriage counselling?)

The authority of God's supposed views depends on accepting that they *are* God's. Most believers see that a violent preacher saying God commands the torture of children would be a fraud or deluded. Their own beliefs about right and wrong have final authority, shaping their view of what God would command. If Holy Books promote horrible views about some other group, or encourage murder or conquering other people's lands, this rightly diminishes their claims. Is a being taking sides in tribal feuds really God? Even if He created the universe and us, He would be an implausible authority on ethics.[7] Where most people value sympathy or mutual respect, society can ignore repellent or ludicrous religious views. The best strategy for peace is not anti-religious. It is gentle but persistent questioning of claimed religious support for violence.

II: 'Unassailable Truth'

Religions have an inspirational side and a dark side. Christianity, a religion of turning the other cheek, was also the religion of Crusades and Inquisition. The dark sides of Judaism and of Islam can support horrible things. This is not just conflicting beliefs, as over the Temple Mount or the Noble Sanctuary. It is about people's rigidity and over-confidence in the 'correctness' of their beliefs. Rebecca Newberger Goldstein brings out that over-confidence in the Inquisition:

It was *an epistemological tragedy, born of men believing themselves to be in firm and indubitable possession of truths that they could not possibly have possessed.*[8] The two different conversations will here illustrate that psychology. One is with a scholarly rabbi trying to justify appalling acts. The other is with a Muslim leader in a regime of horrendous killing and cruelty. Huge numbers of believing Jews and Muslims would be appalled by these extreme variants of their beliefs. No claims are made that the two are equivalent. The interest here is in how beliefs supporting terrible acts can become a closed, self-validating system.

Rigid Judaism: A Scholarly Rabbi

Rabbi Yitzhak Shapira's room had only one picture. It portrayed Rabbi Yitzhak Ginsburgh, who had written: *If a Jew needs a liver can you take the liver of an innocent non-Jew passing by to save him? The Torah would probably permit that. Jewish life has an infinite value. There is something infinitely more holy and unique about Jewish life than non-Jewish life.*[9] Rabbi Shapira's own book supported a similar (not identical) view: *If we kill a Gentile who has sinned or has violated one of the seven commandments – because we care about the commandments – there is nothing wrong with the killing.*[10] Ami Ayalon went to see Rabbi Shapira to understand how Shapira could *find justification where I saw a crime.*[11]

Ayalon explained what he learnt from his parents. He thought Oslo gave Israel a chance to be Jewish and democratic.

The rabbi asked whether Ayalon thought Orthodox Judaism was for or against humanism. Ayalon cited Orthodox Jews – Martin Buber and Rabbi Jonathan Sacks – whose humanism he shared. Rabbi Shapira said supporting land for Palestinians was the opposite of humanism. The Jews were not colonizers. God promised them the land. You cannot colonize what is rightfully yours. *Humanism is about justice and we all know that there can be no contradiction between justice and the Torah. How, then, can justice require the Jewish people to turn against the Torah by betraying the Land of Israel?*[12] The Rabbi was untroubled by doubts. If there is a God, is He likely to have made such a promise? Is there reliable evidence for it? Which of the many versions of justice is humanism 'about'? Which is 'known' to be compatible with the Torah? Do no other values contribute to humanism? Sympathy? Compassion? Kindness? Respect?

Ayalon questioned the Rabbi about a passage in his book: *There are reasons for killing babies even though they have not violated the seven sins, because of the danger that will arise if they are allowed to live and grow up to be as evil as their parents.*[13] Ayalon gives his memory of the conversation:

Now, what is it you don't understand?

Like I said, the bit about killing babies. How do you square that with Thou shalt not kill?

There's nothing to square.

Seems to me there is.

There isn't because, according to the Torah and the consensus of our sages, the absolute prohibition against killing applies only to Jews. The law does not apply to goyim.

Wait! What you're saying is that killing non-Jews is no problem?

According to the Torah, no. The commandment against killing refers to fellow Israelites.[14]

Ayalon summarized what he saw as the Rabbi's view. 'If Jews are fighting against Jews, the biblical prohibition against murder stands. The Gentiles, lacking the light of the Torah, have a different set of rules that places naked self-interest above all else ... International law, the rules of warfare, the Geneva Convention, and the entire history of human rights are window dressing for this elemental egotism.' So, 'only Jews, chosen by God to establish a homeland in the Land of Israel, have carved out a sliver of true morality, and to protect our lives and land we must play by the rules of the goyim.' Ayalon's thought: 'What an upside-down mad hatter's world you inhabit'.[15]

Ayalon admired the Rabbi's modesty and simple life. But *despite his holy airs, Rabbi Shapira terrifies me ... He bases his thinking on religious laws that might have made sense in the Iron Age. But he refuses to update them to include modern conceptions of law and rights.*[16] Ayalon noted that Rabbi Shapira presented his position as a sort of 'unassailable truth',[17] two words perfectly capturing rigidity of belief.

Belief-Based Cruelty: Islamic State

Islamic State, ISIS, had a version of Islam that was in most respects very different from what is accepted by most Palestinians. For its appalling version, ISIS had global ambitions. Defeated in its 'Caliphate' in Iraq and Syria, the ambitions may resurface. It is important for understanding extreme Islamism, though unusual in its degree of cruelty. In one of the 2015 attacks on Paris, some were killed just because they were Jews. ISIS methods include beheadings and burning people alive. The documentary *Islamic State* shows the crucified body of a man on display in a public square. Hard to shake off is a television interview with the mother of a young man they beheaded. They had followed this by the cruelty of giving his head to her.[18] The cruelty 'works' by terrifying. Abu Abdullah al-Muhajjer, in his *Introduction to the Jurisprudence of Jihad*, discusses beheading: *a gory picture ... strengthening the hearts of Muslims and terrorizing the apostates.*[19] Barbarism and cruelty were present at the destruction of Palmyra, a UNESCO World Heritage archaeological site. The 83-year-old Head of Antiquities, Dr Khaled al-Asaad, under weeks of torture refused to say where items were hidden. They beheaded him and displayed his body in public.

Jürgen Todenhöfer is a journalist and a former German judge. In 2014 he interviewed Islamic State leaders.[20] Abu Qatadah, a Sunni Muslim who had grown up in Germany, expected world domination: *We know from the sayings of the Prophet Muhammad that at some point Islam will rule the whole world.*[21] Perhaps the whole world will accept Islam. If not, refusing Christians would be enslaved or killed.

Shias refusing to become Sunnis would not be enslaved: *The Islamic opinion is that Shias are apostates. Their apostasy is their death sentence ... Either they repent and return of their own free will to the true Islam or they will be killed.*

That means if 80 million Iranian, Iraqi and Syrian Shias don't repent and convert to Sunnism of their own free will, they will be killed?

Right. Definitely, yes.

Eighty million?

If it has to be that way. (Laughs.) *I mean that sounds, how can I put it, rather extreme.*[22]

I checked and there are 200 million Shias in the world. You cannot seriously mean you want to eliminate them all if they don't convert to Sunnism, to your true Islam.

What can I say? In the end those are numbers and they are unimaginable for all of us. But as you know, it's easy to kill 6 million or x million, depending on how it's done.[23]

9

BELIEF SYSTEMS: CHALLENGE AND RESPONSE

Conversations outside the charmed circle of like-minded believers can start with talking past each other. One group talks from inside their own beliefs. The other, in a downward spiral, filters through *their* beliefs what they hear. *I understand what you say, but as an Israeli/a Palestinian, you are biased, with wrong assumptions about the conflict.* Or, *because you are a French secularist, you don't understand religion's spiritual nature/because you are a Muslim Jihadi, you don't understand religion's delusional nature.* Even those less confident may think progress on their differences impossible.

This leaves the conversation of mankind underpowered. Belief systems can survive for centuries, even millennia. Confirmation bias, more readily accepting evidence fitting our beliefs than against them, lets us filter out inconvenient experiences or evidence. This only scratches the surface. Deeper down is vast ignorance. Belief systems can be hugely destructive, but few learn to think critically about them. (Like a world ravaged by epidemics where very few study medicine?) To deepen discussions of our differences, we need to understand better how we deceive ourselves about religious and political beliefs. The rigidities assume an impossible infallibility.

I: Conversation with the Confident

Yigal Amir or Abu Qatadah would not question their certainties. Doubts get further in two-way conversation, before minds have hardened solid. Even those reachable can have wildly implausible beliefs. At the mild end of the spectrum, they are 'merely' implausible, as in: *Our version of the conflict is quite correct; theirs is wrong on every point.* Further out, increasingly wild beliefs have greater power to harm:

> *Allah thinks the Jews are untrustworthy.*
> *God promised huge swathes of the Middle East to the Jews.*
> *There's a war coming within a year or two. Then the way will be paved for the Temple.*
> *Our leaders have the right to kill thousands of people in another country to bring regime change.*
> *Those rejecting our religion are rightly targets of terrorism.*
> *Enslaving believers in other religions is acceptable, as is forcing sex on the women.*
> *In Islam, the blood of an unbeliever is basically not protected.*
> *The absolute prohibition on killing applies only to Jews.*

Weakening the grip of 'unassailable truths' is slow. Young Israelis may be more open than senior rabbis who 'know' that any Jewish life matters infinitely more than any non-Jewish life. Questioning jihad may be easier for Muslim students than for Hamas leaders. Those reachable rightly resist being hit over the head with an alternative dogma. 'You think your version of the conflict is right, but it is wrong on every point.' 'Of course, God/Allah said nothing like what your Holy Book claims. Anyway, God/Allah doesn't even exist.' Real persuasion rarely comes from verbal bombing of someone's beliefs. Better gently suggest there are many ways of looking at things; that highly intelligent people hold different views from either of us; perhaps we can learn from people we disagree with. Any of us may struggle for an answer to an objection. Sometimes disagreeing about standards of evidence, can either of us show a third person that our standards are better?

Much indoctrination is religious or political. (Sometimes even for an intolerant anti-religious people. I have not forgotten the revulsion that I, an unbeliever, felt in St Isaac's Cathedral in Leningrad on finding the Soviet authorities had forcibly turned it into a 'museum of atheism'.) One chillingly cruel extreme is the anti-Muslim 're-education' in Chinese concentration camps. Propaganda sometimes retreats before questioning. There is no guarantee, but no reason to lose hope. Weakening rigid certainties needs awareness. How do belief systems take over people's minds? How do they hang together?

II: Beliefs Cluster in Systems

How certain is *any* belief? Are you sure you know what your friend really thinks about you? Is your memory of last year more reliable than your sister's? Can larger religious, political or scientific systems of belief be certain? Can you be sure there is/isn't a God? Is killing people ever right?

Our most successful invention for gaining knowledge is science. But Creationists and others challenge the scientific approach. Some who see a Holy Book as the Word of God think it trumps mere human observation. Others question some of the assumptions of science. Are our senses reliable? Can we move from past observations to theories covering the future? Do we *know* the future will be like the past? Some think science is not a way to judge between beliefs, but is just another ideology, the belief system of the Western-educated world. Yet, science provides ways to decide rationally on many questions about what to believe. It exposes beliefs to potentially hostile evidence. Theories have to be very fit to win the Darwinian struggle to survive.

Distortions can be exposed. Psychologists tease out seductive biases. First cases bias our view of later ones. We are too swayed by cases involving someone famous. Stereotypes influence us more than probabilities.[1] We can correct for these 'local' distortions as we do for visual illusions.

Larger-scale distortions of thought are harder to deal with. Beliefs cluster together in connected systems. When they predict something that does not happen, some may need to be changed. I expect the prescribed medicine will cure my illness. I take it but do not get better. What was I wrong about? I have a wide choice. Perhaps the doctor's skill has declined? Did the pharmacist misread the prescription? Does my chemistry resist that medicine? Other changes are possible. Was I given the wrong medicine as part of a murderous plot? Should I doubt doctors in general? Or should I reject Western medicine, or even the whole scientific method? Some responses are more reasonable, others less so. Beliefs hang together in a system. People making identical false predictions make different choices. Then, in a small way, their belief systems diverge. Over time, the divergences may grow. New information (about the standards doctors have to meet, the frequency of varying responses to medication, etc.) can reduce the area of free play, showing some choices are less reasonable. One belief is not isolated, but part of a system with others, giving great scope to those defending their central religious or political beliefs.

III: Defending the Fixed Point

Any belief *can* be defended by making enough adjustments to the system. The flat earth can be defended by saying there are systematic distortions of light, affecting satellite photographs and creating illusions of ships disappearing over the horizon.

Philip Gosse was a nineteenth-century religious fundamentalist and a scientist working on fossils. He defended Creationism against fossil evidence for evolution. God, to test our faith, planted fossils to look as if evolution had happened. Gosse's failure was not a local one about fossils. It was the pull of a commitment systematically slanting interpretation of relevant evidence. If you have a fixed point (the infallibility of the Torah or the Quran?) you can adjust everything else to fit.

In the 1930s, many joined the British Communist Party because of its anti-Nazi stance. After the Hitler–Stalin pact, Moscow ordered the British Party to oppose the war against Nazism: perhaps even working for Britain's defeat. In the Party's Central Committee's debate, some accepted this against all their anti-Nazi convictions. *Their* fixed point was that the Soviet Union was always right. The new policy would be easier to accept if the democracies were as bad as Nazi Germany. (One said British colonialism was worse than Nazi concentration camps. Another saw *little to choose between Hitler and Chamberlain*.) The policy would be easier if Germany was no threat. (In three years, Hitler had occupied the Rhineland, taken over Austria and part of Czechoslovakia, and successfully invaded Poland.) One said that *the plain fact is not the power of Germany but the weakness of Germany*. Another said a weak Germany was *desperately searching for peace*.[2]

Defending the Fixed Point When Prophecy Fails

When the medicine does not cure me, it is not hard to choose which beliefs to query. My chemistry not responding to the medicine, or some slip-up over the prescription are fairly plausible. Rejecting all scientific medicine is not. It is more difficult, and more interesting, if a failed prediction seriously threatens core beliefs.

Some groups' fixed point has been the imminent end of the world. When that does not come, some cling to belief even more firmly. In the 1950s Leon Festinger and colleagues studied the hold of these falsified beliefs.[3] 'Mrs Marian Keech' (not her real name) had messages from 'superior beings' on flying saucers, saying fault lines they saw in the earth's crust would cause disastrous flooding. In Mrs Keech's hometown, earthquakes would destroy tall buildings and a wave from the lake would cover the city and flow to the Gulf of Mexico.

Mrs Keech's group waited at her house for their promised flying saucer rescue. Days after the predicted one there were no earthquakes, flood or rescue. They still seemed to believe, giving press interviews aiming at new converts. When fixed beliefs conflict with overwhelming evidence, one interpretation sees their belief as insecure, so the group is left muddled and confused. The more interesting interpretation is that they cannot give up their belief, as in the British Communist Party debate in World War II. 'True believers' search for any support, however unlikely. Perhaps the group hoped telepathy had malfunctioned, changing the date of the otherwise correct prediction?

Defending the Fixed Point When the 'Impossible' Happens

> *And I will bring again the captivity of my people of Israel,*
> *and they shall build the waste cities and inhabit them, and*
> *they shall plant vineyards, and drink the wine thereof, they*
> *shall also make gardens, and eat the fruit of them. And I will*
> *plant them again upon their land, and they shall no more be*
> *pulled up out of their land which I have given them, saith the*
> *Lord thy God.*
> AMOS, Chapter nine, verses 14–15, King James translation.

Rabbi Zvi Yehuda Kook was not trying to explain a failed prophecy. He thought a prophecy was confirmed. Amos said the Jewish people would be restored to the Promised Land and never again uprooted. Rabbi Kook interpreted Israel's 1967 victory: *Thanks to God, the Prophetic visions are unfolding before our very eyes. There is no more room for doubt or any question that might rattle our joy and gratitude to the Redeemer of Israel.*[4] God made withdrawing from any of the captured territory impossible. Some have clarified this, saying withdrawal was not 'forbidden', but God's decision meant it *could* not happen. Micah Goodman explained the view of Rabbi Kook and of the settler Hanan Porat: *withdrawal from any part of the land of Israel was simply metaphysically impossible – and to believe it might actually happen was nothing but superstition.* He quotes Rabbi Yaakov Filber: *we have to teach ourselves that the notion of withdrawal is every bit as fantastical as ghosts.*[5]

Rabbi Kook did not have to explain a failed prophecy. He died just before the 1982 final evacuation of the Jewish settlements in the Sinai desert. Some would have expected evacuation to destroy this version of religious Zionism. Micah Goodman says, *there was certainly a crisis, but the messianic school of history survived the first event that was supposed to discredit it.* A later crisis was more serious. In 2005, Israeli settlers were evacuated from the Gaza Strip. Many in Gush Katif settlement refused to prepare for evacuation. Some (relying on metaphysics?) said it would never happen. But it did. Some followers thought perhaps Rabbi Kook was wrong. Others tried to save the prophecy: *the stages of withdrawal and crisis are also part of our journey and ascent ... training and preparation for the next stage of the Salvation.*

Do belief systems adjusting to defend a fixed point make discussion with true believers (whether followers of Mrs Keech or Rabbi Kook) pointless? Does it mean that there is no way to weaken any very strongly committed person's system of beliefs? Or, at some stage, does defending a fixed point by adjusting everything else become absurdly implausible? God planting the fossils to test our faith? A weak Nazi Germany desperately searching for peace? The flying saucer rescue delayed? Thinking of giving up Gaza settlements as fantastic as belief in ghosts?

IV: From Rigid Certainty to Degrees of Plausibility

Ideology, political or religious, is usually kept away from philosophical questions about what we can know. Many believers think our great confidence in everyday common sense extends to their own political or religious beliefs. But 'God promised the land to us' or 'Allah thinks Jews cannot be trusted' are not obviously plausible candidates. How *do* we decide how plausible a belief is? The obvious starting point: the more evidence that supports a belief, and the less against it, the more plausible it is. But how much weight should different bits of evidence – or different *kinds* of evidence – have?

There are obvious disagreements. Much of the 'feel' for plausibility comes from two overlapping sources. One is a set of 'framework' principles used in accepting or rejecting beliefs. This framework may come from personal experience of what principles have been more or less reliable. Or it may come from science, religion or some other general outlook. But, before any worked-out principles, plausibility is often judged by already embedded beliefs we are unaware of. I don't notice my belief that cows can't fly until someone says they saw a cow circling above London.

Embedded Beliefs

Alison Gopnik draws on research showing how much starts before adult teaching embeds other beliefs. *An animal that depends on the accumulated knowledge of past generations has to have some time to acquire that knowledge. An animal that depends on imagination has to have some time to exercise it. Childhood is that time. Children are protected from the usual exigencies of adult life; they don't need to hunt deer or ward off sabre-toothed tigers ... All they need to do is learn ... We adults are just the final products of childhood. Our brains are the brains that were shaped by experience, our lives are the lives that began as babies, our consciousness is the consciousness that reaches back to childhood.*[6]

Early imagination shapes babies' ideas of the world. Embedded beliefs are an anchoring context for others. Ludwig Wittgenstein thought we cannot seriously question some of them: *The truth of certain empirical propositions belongs to our frame of reference.*[7] Such a belief may be *anchored in all my questions and answers, so anchored that I cannot touch it.* Perhaps it is too quick to say any particular embedded belief cannot be questioned. A mistake of Wittgenstein's brings this out. *If we are thinking within our system, then it is certain that no-one has ever been to the moon. Not merely is nothing of the sort ever seriously reported to us by reasonable people, but our whole system forbids us to believe it. For this demands answers to the questions, 'How did he overcome the force of gravity?' 'How could he live without an atmosphere?' and a thousand others which could not be answered.*[8] This was in 1950, only nineteen years before the first moon landing.

We *can* question more embedded beliefs than Wittgenstein thought. They often come from trusted people. But this can go wrong. The distinguished philosopher Allen Buchanan was a mid-twentieth-century child in the segregated Deep South of the United States. *I was taught by explicit dogma and by example to regard Blacks as sub-human. Unlike my mother, I never witnessed a lynching, but I did once see a desiccated severed black ear ... proudly displayed by a white junior high school classmate.* He also joked about the 'Tucker telephone', used in a penal institution to give electric shocks to Black people's genitals. Buchanan came to see all this as based on false beliefs about racial differences. *Those I had trusted and looked up to – my parents, aunts and uncles, pastor, teachers, and local government officials – had been sources of dangerous error, not truth.*[9]

Knowledge and belief are a shared enterprise. We cannot all be experts on quantum theory. Many of us have little clue about what to do when the computer crashes. We accept the authority of others. But on social or political matters there is danger of being misled as Buchanan was. Sometimes, as with racism, indoctrination imposes negative stereotypes. There is no single antidote. But hostile propaganda is less effective if children of different groups live mixed together, make friends and are encouraged to talk to each other.

Where embedded beliefs are widely shared, they can seem so obvious that no reasons are needed. 'It is not rocket science', or 'It is just common sense'. But untheoretical common sense does not explain. Our thoughts make sense only against a background of accepted beliefs. But we cannot assume that any particular belief is *'so anchored that I cannot touch it'*. The history of physics and other sciences includes the overthrow of embedded beliefs that seemed too anchored to touch (the flat earth, the sun going round it, man as a separate creation from animals, etc.). Einstein is reported to have described common sense as a deposit of prejudices laid down before the age of eighteen. The novelist and art critic John Berger wrote: *Common-sense is part of the home-made ideology of those who have been deprived of fundamental learning ... compounded from different sources: items that have survived from religion, items of empirical knowledge, items of protective scepticism ... But the point is that common-sense can never teach itself, can never advance beyond its own limits ... Common-sense can only exist as a category insofar as it can be distinguished from the spirit of enquiry, from philosophy.*[10]

Embedded Categories and Threatened Boundaries

Not only embedded *beliefs* harden into rigid certainties. So can embedded *categories*. Rational thought includes making category boundaries clearer. Sometimes it means loosening

their grip. Twentieth-century anthropologists wrote sugges-
tively about the basis of food taboos. Edmund Leach saw
foods forbidden to Jews in Leviticus as anomalies breaching
category boundaries coming from Genesis. On the fifth
day, God created fish and birds. On the sixth He made
domestic cattle and wild animals. That day He also created
the anomalous 'creeping things': neither fish nor fowl, and
not animals like cows or sheep. These 'abominations' were
forbidden food. Other anomalies straddle other boundaries:
'water creatures with no fins, animals and birds which eat no
meat or fish'. (Leach pointed out that the Israelites did eat
locusts, so an exception allowed creeping things whose legs
let them leap above earth.[11])

Another anthropologist, Mary Douglas, followed Leach
on these taboos but later saw God's command to be holy as
central. That included being complete or whole. A holy man
must be physically and mentally complete: *holiness is unity,
integrity, perfection of the individual and of the kind. The
dietary rules merely develop the metaphor of holiness on the
same lines.*[12] Perhaps. But there are rival explanations. In
a hot climate, are these foods a health risk? Mary Douglas
dismissed 'medical materialism'. *It is one thing to point out
the side benefits of ritual actions, and another thing to be
content with using the by-products as a sufficient explanation.
Even if some of Moses's dietary rules were hygienically
beneficial, it is a pity to treat him as an enlightened public
health administrator, rather than as a spiritual leader.*[13] This
just assumed the health benefits were mere 'side effects' or
'by-products', Her later view was (slightly) more open. *There
is no objection to this approach* (medical materialism) *unless
it excludes other interpretations.*[14]

Many defend threatened category boundaries. Were
opponents of Darwin defending *only* God's role in creation?
Evolution challenged also the deep boundary between humans
and (other) animals. Gender boundaries may be another
case. Could hostility to homosexuality have come from its
challenging deep boundaries between men's and women's
expected sexuality? Could anger expressed on transgender
issues be a response to similar challenges? In the abortion
debate, important values are at stake: preserving human life
versus freedom from invasive denials of women's autonomy.

But there are fiercely contested rival boundaries of the start of human moral status. Does boundary-blurring make these debates so overheated?

V: Rival Frameworks as Separation Walls of the Mind?

Plausibility estimates can come from framework principles. Laying down methods to assess beliefs, they control how a system hangs together. They usually include rules of logic and basic scientific standards for interpreting evidence. They may be followed intuitively by naturally good scientists who do not reflect on method, or by bright children. Framework principles are the load-bearing walls of the house. Changing them may threaten the whole system. Debating evolution versus creationism is different when the ground rules do or do not include consistency with a Holy Book.

Basic logic is relatively uncontroversial. So, on quantitative issues, are principles of statistics. Other principles are more debated. 'Accept the simpler explanation'. (Always? And what counts as 'simpler'?) Some framework principles are 'axioms', the Supreme Court of a belief system: *We all know there can be no contradiction between justice and the Torah.* Cardinal Newman said about his Catholic beliefs that *ten thousand difficulties do not make one doubt.*[15] The problem is that we disagree about framework principles too. Does this mean that, like a mental version of the Israel–Palestine separation wall, they stop us communicating with each other?

Rival Frameworks: Can We Talk to Each Other?

People disagreeing may be using different categories and concepts. Is useful discussion possible? Some rightly think that, if we disagree with each other's beliefs and concepts, theirs cannot be *utterly* different from ours. Some things said in each 'language' can be translated into the other, indicating some shared 'basic' framework. But this allows more modest 'local' frameworks to diverge. Those who say 'a woman's right to choose' and those who say 'murder of the unborn child' have rival 'local' frameworks. But a shared basic framework allows debate with each other. The same for rival conceptions of 'Israel' and 'Palestine'.

Some pessimists say *fruitful* discussion is impossible: that would need a shared *local* framework. Karl Popper thought this pessimistic view harmful, perhaps replacing dialogue by violence and war. He thought Western civilization started when the Greeks saw the rival claims of Egyptian, Persian and other religions could not all be true. They turned from teaching religion as dogma to critical discussion.[16] (I wonder how far the evidence supports this encouraging conjecture?) Dialogue is easier if both sides accept platitudes of rationality: vary degree of belief with the strength of reasons given, etc. But many change framework principles to defend their views. Doubting Thomas, rebuked for doubting the resurrection until he saw Christ, is propaganda for the view that it is *better* to believe without evidence.

Can We Decide Between Frameworks?

Interpretating evidence in psychiatry is not the same as in physics. Some framework principles, such as rules of logic, claim universality. Others fit only their context. Where there is disagreement on framework principles, is that because, like chemists before the Periodic Table, we have not yet found the map? Or are there no 'best' framework principles?

Some children notice: *If I lived 200 years ago, in China, I would think different thoughts.* One reason for modesty: our own beliefs come partly from things in our lives that could have been different. Many have hoped to find non-parochial objective truth. In philosophy, Descartes wanted to make a completely fresh start, doubting his whole belief system and rebuilding it on secure foundations. Now, 'new foundations' for a belief system seem less desirable. A platitude of modern philosophy is that you cannot give up *all* your beliefs and still rebuild your system. Looking for new foundations, there have to be reasons for choosing some, not others. Aren't those reasons just beliefs again?

'New foundations' sounds like rebuilding a house. Perhaps this is not the best model. In Otto Neurath's famous image, *we are like sailors who on the open sea have to reconstruct their ship but are never able to start afresh from the bottom. Where a beam is taken away, a new one must at once be put there, and for this the rest of the ship is used in support. In this way, by using the old beams and driftwood the ship can be shaped entirely anew, but only by gradual reconstruction.*[17] This liberating image leaves us still disagreeing about what needs replacing. What we build depends on which beliefs (old or newly adopted) we start from.

Results will be small if we start only with axioms we cannot doubt. A more fruitful start may be with the scientific picture of the world. That supports the general reliability of our senses. A species with senses that mainly gave wrong information about the world would probably not survive. Keeping afloat these large bits of the ship is more promising than keeping only a few planks.

Critics rightly point out the circularity. The scientific world picture, including evolution, rests on the evidence of our senses. This defence of our senses depends on evolution. Is our whole system of knowledge really based on this circular reasoning? If the boat picture is right, some circularity is unavoidable. We have to keep some beliefs afloat to look critically at others. Inevitably the framework principles and the beliefs about the world we end up with will be in mutual support. Having such support need not stop us criticizing some beliefs as irrational, nor from sometimes having good reasons for doing so.

Intellectual Costs of Different Cognitive Strategies

Our framework principles reflect our own history and experience. But there are rational ways to discuss our differences. They start with people spelling out their beliefs and their reasons for them. Next is evidence against the beliefs or counter-examples to the reasons. 'Are you really prepared to accept *this* implication of what you say?' Beliefs are opposed by showing their intellectual costs. Implausible consequences invite a change of belief. Logic can exclude belief systems that depend on fallacies or are inconsistent. But logic is not enough to choose between rival consistent ones.

In ideological conflicts, many disagree on their fixed points. Does this make discussion futile: a game of cards where players choose their own trumps? Or could agreement be reached that some cognitive strategies are better than others? We can work out the costs of holding some particular belief. We can also work out the intellectual costs of a cognitive strategy. People who think aliens abducted them are bad at answering detailed questions. They sometimes say they have forgotten: the aliens erased their memories.[18] Few are impressed. And few are impressed by Gosse waving away the fossil evidence for evolution, or by the response to doubts about the 1939 new Communist Party line. If you show my defence of a cherished belief is exactly parallel to one of these ploys, you undermine it. Absurd consequences discredit particular beliefs. They discredit cognitive strategies too.

I do not believe there is a God. Perhaps you do. Suppose we are both good enough at reasoning to avoid obviously absurd consequences. We each explain in our own terms what we see as the weakness of the other's position. I may give reasons to find unconvincing the claimed support for God's existence. You may see me as blind to spiritual dimensions reached by parts of us other than the intellect. When we have both made our case, I still stick to atheism and you still stick to belief. We needn't lose respect for each other. Neither need think the other stupid. If we are wise, neither will think our own view is *unassailable* truth.

Beliefs leading Catholics and Protestants to kill each other in the Thirty Years War don't seem unassailable to many now. Fewer Europeans are utterly certain that this or that religion uniquely is true, or that religious belief is worth killing for. Aggressive certainties can yield a bit to scepticism. Loosening rigid beliefs is slow. But societies hoping to live at peace should not give up on it. Growing up includes mutually adjusting both culturally embedded beliefs and rival framework principles. If both sides remember this, rival frameworks may no longer be a barrier. They may start sounding like an interesting part of the conversation of mankind.

The Ruined House of Certainty

Those of us teaching philosophy sometimes wish that, wanting to say what we think we have learnt, we had the human reach of a poet's voice. We have to borrow:

From the place where we are right
Flowers will never grow in the spring.
The place where we are right
Is hard and trampled
Like a yard.
But doubts and loves
Dig up the world
Like a mole, a plough.
And a whisper will be heard in the place
Where the ruined
House once stood.
YEHUDA AMICHAI: *The Place Where We are Right.*

In *good* conversations about political or religious beliefs, people rarely claim certainty. Questions are unthreatening. They are about whether a convincing case can be made to others, a dialogue a bit like philosophy. (Does that mean it is *infinitely* slow, interminable? But those of us who think about philosophy do sometimes see its gradual effects on ourselves or on others.) A softly worded challenge does not usually make people converge on 'unassailable' answers. There may be objections not yet considered. Uncertainty may come from not knowing how to answer a question. Seeing how precarious a view is may create more awareness of alternatives. Sometimes we change our minds, not always in the same direction. We adapt or even leave our house of belief (whether the one we first lived in or one rebuilt on foundations we thought secure). Reduced confidence suggests a different tone, letting a whisper be heard where the ruined house once stood. A tone not welcomed by terrorist recruiters, by religious assassins, or by politicians loudly drumming up support for a war. Critical thinking may greatly damage a house built on unassailable truth. Those who lived there may feel it has become a bit of a ruin. But, if flowers do grow there, a good thing too.

10
IDENTITY TRAPS

It was in 1940s Yugoslavia that Rebecca West saw our tribal wars as a suicidal tendency we are in denial about: *Sometimes we search for peace, sometimes we make an effort to find convenient frontiers and a proper fulfilment for racial destinies; but sometimes we insist on war, sometimes we stamp into the dust the only foundations on which we can support our national lives. We ignore this suicidal strain in history because we are consistently bad artists when we paint ourselves.*[1]

The Israel–Palestine conflict has wounded so many for so long. Has each side's identity been shaped by the mutual bitterness, making them stamp into the dust the only foundations of peace? If people detach themselves from hostile narratives, does this betray the self-portraits they have painted?

I: Conflict-Shaped Identity

For twelve years the Olive Tree Programme at London's City University supported Palestinian–Israeli student dialogue about the conflict. Some had vivid experience, losing someone close or suffering post-traumatic stress. Some were taken to meet former activists and paramilitaries in Northern Ireland.

Dialogue reconciling differences was the unfulfilled hope. The programme nearly collapsed.

The new director, Rosemary Hollis, lowered its aim to teaching how rival narratives reinforce conflict. Her thought was that *Our national narratives, with the plot lines and character roles already sketched out for us when we are born ... become drivers or imperatives to act, and react, to others ... it is in this sense that the actors in a conflict can become trapped by their narratives ... unable to detach themselves sufficiently to separate from it.* Her hypothesis for the course was that *groups can become so trapped in their respective narratives that they cannot define themselves except in distinction from the other.*[2]

Students explored values in childhood nursery rhymes and fairy tales, readily seeing links between stories leaving strong messages and the imprint of national narratives.[3] A pair of Palestinian students or a pair of Israeli students would research and present a key episode in the conflict, giving their side's narrative, without their own opinions. Rosemary Hollis thought this the most potent part of the course: *they had a new appreciation of the coexistence of several internally coherent, deeply held and fundamentally incompatible narratives.*[4] Asked about the other side, the Israelis moved more towards understanding Palestinians than Palestinians did towards them. Some accounts biased towards their own side came from each group. Some Palestinians claimed ancestors living in the land of Canaan before Jews came. Some included inner conflict. *I'm supposed to consider the Israelis as two opposing things. On the one side they are the other whose existence prolongs the occupation and on the other side some of them are my friends who love and respect me.*[5]

Hollis said each *can* escape the hostile narratives – but at a price. *It began to dawn on everyone, myself included, that to ask someone to relinquish or fundamentally revise their own narrative is to ask them to reconsider their own identity. That is a very big ask – it is undermining, disorienting, and potentially alarming.* So, interlocutors *must understand the enormity of what is at stake ... if they dig deep enough to come to grips with the core elements in the conflict.*[6] Understanding the conflict *does* mean digging that deep. But weakening its grip requires seeing the huge costs of giving full weight to the rival view. Should Israeli–Palestinian dialogues share thoughts on identity problems raised by that 'very big ask' and how is it possible to cope with them?

Where do they come from, these identities that have such a hold?

Identity as a Muslim, as an Arab, as a Palestinian

Palestinian identity is shaped by more than the current conflict. It has religious, ethnic and national elements, sometimes shaped by wounds known only through folk memory.

Muslim Memory of the Crusades Across a Thousand Years: Maarat An-Numan, 1098–1099

Crusaders besieged the town. Defenders, stripping the country and blocking the wells, left them no food or water. The Crusader commander agreed to spare the defenders. They stopped fighting. But Crusader atrocity included killing huge numbers, enslaving others and allowing inhabitants water only if they paid.

In a flood, grain rotted. Bread floated away. Desperate Crusaders ate decomposing Saracen corpses. Albert of Aachen said they ate dead Turks and Saracens and even dogs. Robert the Monk said they ate cut-up Turkish bodies. The anonymous *Gesta Francorum* agreed. So did Raymond of Aguilers. Fulcher of Chartres said cooked pieces of dead Saracens were *devoured with savage mouth*.[7] Five converging accounts may well be true.

The *Chanson d'Antioch* account seems to go further. It includes: *Forced to eat donkeys and horses, they even ate Turks, and some killed them* [killing to eat them?]. In another account, Ralph of Caen implied that people were cooked alive. *I heard that living people heard that they said that they were forced by the lack of food to begin to eat human flesh. Adults from among the gentiles were put into the cooking pot and their youth were fixed on spits and roasted. In devouring them the Christians looked like wild beasts, like dogs roasting men.*[8] Eating corpses violates a deep taboo. But killing people for food is much worse. Cooking people alive adds another dimension of horror.

Were people killed to be eaten? *Were* people cooked alive? The more extreme suggestions of Ralph of Caen are not supported by other accounts. And Ralph was not a witness: *I heard that living people heard that they said that … Over centuries stories grow.* Amin Maalouf, a Lebanese Christian with Muslim sympathies, in his book *The Crusades through Arab Eyes*, quotes Ralph's more extreme account. He includes this version of a sentence quoted above: *In Ma'rra our troops boiled pagan adults in cooking-pots; they impaled children on spits and devoured them grilled.* Maalouf seems to accept the extreme version: *The Frankish chronicles of the epoch contain numerous accounts of the acts of cannibalism committed by the Frankish armies in Ma'rra in 1098, and they all agree. Until the nineteenth century, the facts of these events were included in the works of European historians. In the twentieth century, however, these accounts have generally been concealed – perhaps in the interests of the West's 'civilizing mission'?*[9] Perhaps. But later historians may have doubted the reliability of Ralph of Caen's version. Or noticed that the Frankish accounts do not 'all agree' with his version?

There were appalling atrocities: the massacre – after promising to spare lives; torture and enslavement; blocking access to water. Maalouf may well be right that *the memory of these atrocities, preserved and transmitted by local poets and oral tradition, shaped an image of the Frank that would not easily fade … The Ma'rra incident was to contribute to opening a chasm between the Arabs and the Franks that would not be bridged for centuries to come.*[10]

The Capture of Jerusalem, 1099

In 638, Christian Jerusalem surrendered to the Muslims. In 1099, Crusaders recaptured it. Albert of Aachen described the atrocities: *The Christian victors, after the very great and cruel slaughter of the Saracens, of whom ten thousand fell … were piercing through with the sword's point women who had fled into the turreted palaces and dwellings, seizing by the soles of their feet from their mothers' laps or their cradles infants who were still suckling and dashing them against the walls or lintels of the doors and breaking their necks.*[11] It also was part of the history of Jews as victims. They all fled to the main synagogue and were inside when the Crusaders burnt it down. No Muslims or Jews were left in Jerusalem. Muslims contrast the Crusader capture of Jerusalem with Saladin's Muslim recapture of it without injuries or deaths.

Bitter Memories?

In 2001, Osama bin Laden wrote about the Afghanistan war: *Is it a single, unrelated event, or is it part of a long series of Crusader wars against the Islamic world? Since World War One ... the entire Islamic world has fallen under the Crusader banners, under the British, French and Italian governments. They divided up the whole world between them ... We should therefore see events not as isolated incidents, but as part of a long chain of conspiracies, a war of annihilation in all senses of the word.*[12] How far the Crusades still live in Muslim memory is debated. Jonathan Riley-Smith is a sceptic: *One often reads that the Muslims have inherited from their medieval ancestors bitter memories of the violence of the Crusaders. Nothing could be further from the truth. Muslims had not hitherto shown much interest in the Crusades ... The writing of Crusade history among them originated in the 1890s, when the Ottoman Empire was in crisis.*[13] Paul Cobb puts the other case: *... the Crusades did live on in Muslim historical memory ... in the silent, immovable presence of castles, walls and ruins linked – sometimes by name – to a region's own experience with the Franks ... Historical memory does not always abide in scholarly books and articles.*[14]

Figure 8: Krak des Chevaliers, al-Husn

Memories of Colonialism: The Sykes–Picot Agreement

Most frontiers in Africa today are arbitrary, not reflecting boundaries of different ethnic or cultural groups. They reflect regions that colonial powers conquered or deals they did with each other. Britain and France, in a similar if less arbitrary way, established new borders in the Middle East after the First World War. The first attempt was infamously part of a 1916 agreement between Sir Mark Sykes and Francois Picot, creating (French-ruled) Syria and (British-ruled) Iraq. The agreement was never put into effect. Different borders were established after the war. But Sykes–Picot remains a popular, if misleading, symbol of Western intervention. In a 2014 documentary, *Islamic State*, Isis guides drove a Western film crew across the Iraq–Syria border. The gun-toting jihadi made an unexpected historical reference.

Figure 9: ISIS militant
Jerusalem Post

So, later, did Osama bin Laden, speaking of *the Sykes– Picot agreement between France and Britain, which brought about the dissection of the Islamic world into fragments. … In the light of a new Sykes–Picot agreement, the Bush–Blair axis, which has the same banner and objective, namely the banner of the cross and the objective of destroying and looting our beloved Prophet's umma.*[15]

Palestinian Experience of the Conflict with Israel

From the window you see
Hills of olive trees
Bereft of their ancient peace of mind ...

From the window
you see in the sky
a thunderous hunk of metal
with complacent wings and an unerring aim,
circling as it hunts for its next target
(could it be the woman in mourning?).
It pursues her
beneath the threatened domes, it pins her against her
  bedroom wall
(where the picture of her absent son
Fixes his last smile in black and white).
From MOURID BARGHOUTI: *Midnight*, translated by Radwa Ashour.

Identity as a Jew, as an Israeli

For centuries antisemitism and the associated persecutions relied on a hotch-potch of 'reasons'. 'The Jews killed Christ', or Jews ritually murdered Christians to use their blood in Passover bread. Claims that a boy of nine was ritually murdered in Lincoln led to 91 Jews being sent to the Tower of London, with 18 of them executed. Auto-da-fe, forced public penance by 'heretics' (mainly Jews), often led to them being burnt alive. More recent antisemitic stereotypes included 'the Jews' as both greedy financiers and communists.

Many found wearing the Nazi-imposed yellow star a form of torture, like being branded. The idea went back at least as far as Thomas Aquinas: *you ask whether it is good that Jews throughout your province are compelled to wear a sign distinguishing them from Christians ... Jews of each sex in all Christian provinces, and all the time, should be distinguished from other people by some clothing.*[16] Martin Luther went further: *What shall we do with this rejected and condemned people, the Jews? – set fire to their synagogues or schools ... I advise that their houses also be razed and destroyed ... I advise that their rabbis be forbidden to*

*teach ... on pain of loss of life and limb ... Our rulers must
act like a good physician who, when gangrene has set in,
proceeds without mercy to cut and saw.*[17]

In *The Merchant of Venice*, the pound of flesh demanded
in Shylock's contract was revenge for Antonio's antisemitism: *it will feed my revenge; he hath disgraced me
... laughed at my losses, mock'd at my gains, scorned
my Nation, thwarted my bargains, cooled my friends,
heated mine enemies, and what's his reason? I am a Jew.*
Shakespeare put truths into Shylock's mouth: *Hath not a
Jew eyes? Hath not a Jew hands, organs, dimensions, senses,
affections, passions, fed with the same food, hurt with the
same weapons, subject to the same diseases, healed by the
same means, warmed and cooled by the same winter and
summer as a Christian is: if you prick us do we not bleed? If
you tickle us do we not laugh? If you poison us do we not
die?*[18] But truths rarely reach those determined not to hear.

The Holocaust

DEATH FUGUE
*Black milk of daybreak we drink you at night
We drink you at noon death is a master from Germany
We drink you at sundown and in the morning we drink and
     we drink you
death is a master from Germany his eyes are blue
he strikes you with leaden bullets his aim is true
a man lives in the house your golden hair Margarete
he sets his pack on us he grants us a grave in the air
he plays with the serpents and daydreams death is a master
     from Germany*

*your golden hair Margarete
your ashen hair Shulamith*

From PAUL CELAN: *Todesfuge,* translated by Michael
Hamburger.

Identity as an Israeli

Jewish identity is not all about antisemitism, persecution and
genocide. The history is rich in sources of pride. Mankind's

simplest and deepest poetry includes the Psalms and Isaiah. The Bible says Ruth and Boaz were the great-grandparents of King David. Their story is a simple and sublime account of kindness bridging a gulf between people of different tribes. It is not only the Bible. The legal tradition from the Torah shaped the Jewish argumentativeness, religious and secular, that Amos Oz loved.

My philosophical colleague Anthony Quinton once asked how different religions have or haven't helped people look through the surface of things to underlying causes. He gave the prize to Christianity over Hinduism or Confucianism. My response was that, in any contest over whose believers (or whose secular grandchildren) have done most to look beneath the surface of things, Judaism would deserve to be at least a finalist. Einstein, Marx, Freud and Wittgenstein would not be a bad opening bid.[19]

After the past glories and tragedies, how could history not shape Jews' Israeli identity? Sometimes it is a matter of continuity. Anyone knowing Israel can see how vigorously alive is the Jewish love of discussion and argument. Sometimes it is a matter of pride at having escaped aspects of the past. This can include a degree of pride that, when a cluster of neighbouring countries were at war with the new state, Israel won decisively. Jews need not be victims.

II: Identity Transcending the Conflict

The world can often see the strengths of Palestinian and Israeli identities. It can also see the horrors committed by both sides. For both nations, peace might let them escape constant pressure to justify their own side's actions. A burden many are used to, but whose shedding may be a greater relief than they expect.

It is very unlikely that an Oslo-type agreement will soon bring peace. Alternatives move away from negotiations towards relationships and psychology. They may be frustrated by links between the conflict and people's identities. Even if there is hope, and at this stage it *is* only hope, it may take decades rather than a century or more. But 'hope' is not just empty rhetoric. In identity-laden conflict, peace comes partly from gradual changes in how peoples see themselves and their opponents.

Seventeenth-century European religious wars also displayed strong identities. They cared so deeply that many would accept being tortured to death rather than abandon who they were by changing religion. The Jesuit missionary to Protestant England, Edmund Campion, made a statement in the brief interlude between being tortured on the rack and his execution: *Be it known to you that we have made a league – all the Jesuits in the world, cheerfully to carry the cross you shall lay upon us, and never to despair of your recovery, while we have a man left to enjoy your Tyburn, or to be racked with your torments or consumed with your prisons.*[20] The Thirty Years War, despite being between different states and rulers, was very roughly between Catholics and Protestants. Often their identity was shot through with religious commitments as strong as Campion's. Even Northern Irish Catholics and Protestants in the 1980s had only ghostly religious passions compared to that. Over time, and certainly over generations, identity commitments can shift and fade. May the Israel–Palestine version take a lifetime or less, not generations. Either way, the sooner the better.

III: Indoctrination or *Self*-Creation?

States, religions and political movements sometimes try to shape people's values and identities. Bernard Avishai gives a very critical account – no doubt many would disagree – of Haredi schools in Israel: *More than 45% of schoolchildren in Greater Jerusalem are now Haredi ... Haredi schools are closed, rather cultish affairs ... They ... often seem in positive fear of western liberal humanities ... there are rarely secular studies and no computer training. The boys learn the mind-bending techniques of scholastic rabbinic debate, but are not exposed to what would pass for critical thinking.*[21]

Indoctrination often works. But John Stuart Mill strongly expressed the appeal of the alternative: *He who lets the world, or his own portion of it, choose his plan of life for him, has no need of any other faculty than the ape-like one of imitation ... Human nature is not a machine to be built after a model ... but a tree, which requires to grow and develop itself on all sides, according to the tendency of the inward forces which make it a living thing.*[22] This alternative lets identity and beliefs come partly from *self*-creation, from responses (rational and emotional) to experience, including conversation. Iltezam Morrar, meeting Israeli activists taking part in non-violent protests in Budrus, stopped seeing Israelis through a stereotype: *I did not think that one day I would have Israeli friends or even talk to Israeli women ... They don't really hate us.* The contrast with indoctrination is sharp. Children's education includes talk about their different ways of seeing things, learning to question, think for themselves and disagree without enmity. Shouldn't this start early?

The Potential of Shared Education: Lunel

Young Muslims, often alienated within countries where they lived, carried out jihadi atrocities against Europe. Lunel, a run-down town near Montpellier, where drug dealers had replaced shopkeepers, became 'the capital of French jihad'. By 2018, twenty men had left to fight in Syria. Eight were killed. Gilles Kepel, a Professor of Political Science at the *École Normale Supérieure*,[23] found a quarter to a third of its people were North African Muslims with nearly 40 per cent of their young people unemployed. One young Muslim, arrested as a suspected jihadi, mentioned discrimination. Of the class doing the accountancy degree, all the native French found jobs but the two Arabs did not. No networks in the town link Muslims with others. The big new Mosque was fertile for Islamist recruiting.

But one impressive school taught students from both sides in a secular atmosphere. It was the Lycée Louis Feuillade, near the low-income housing the jihadis came from. After the terrorist attacks on Charlie Hebdo, the lycée ran discussions. Some students had hashtags supporting either the magazine or the attacks. Gilles Kepel was still able to write: *I have retained the image of a single place where all the city's components live together in a 'friendship' ... that allows them, through work and shared values, to move beyond atavism and communalism: the lycée.*[24]

Northern Ireland: Moving Towards Integrated Schools

During the Northern Irish troubles, a university student told me about one stereotype. Coming from warring communities, students wanted friends across the barriers. To hide which side they came from, they used only first names, revealing less than surnames. After making friends, they would happily talk across the barrier, including about their backgrounds. The woman talking to me was surprised to hear one childhood stereotype on the other side about her community, who were said to display their lower form of humanity. Instead of two separate eyebrows, they had one long one running above both eyes. Her surprise was that it was the same stereotype *she* as a girl had been told about *them*. The ludicrous slur, believable only by very young children, depended on segregated schooling.

In a 1987 Irish Republican Army funeral, a salute was fired over the coffins. The Royal Irish Constabulary then fired plastic bullets into the crowd, causing injuries. A week later, the Provisional IRA exploded a huge bomb at the Enniskillen Remembrance Day service commemorating British and Northern Irish soldiers killed in war. It killed eleven people and injured more than sixty, including children. One man died after thirteen years in a coma. Revulsion was widespread in the Irish Republic as well as the UK. In Northern Ireland it was widely felt among Catholic Nationalists as well as Protestant Unionists. The IRA apologized, saying they had intended to kill 'only' British soldiers. The cycle of violence continued with a week of fourteen Protestant gun and bomb attacks on Catholics in Belfast.[25]

The climate in Enniskillen is different now. Schooling has changed. There are two integrated institutions: Enniskillen Integrated Primary School and Erne Integrated College. The ethos comes across in the 'Welcome' by Erne College's Principal: *As an integrated school we celebrate diversity and believe it enriches our society. We actively encourage students from all religious traditions, all nationalities and abilities to attend our school in order to work and learn together in an atmosphere of mutual respect and acceptance of difference.*[26]

Integration in education has been slow. One poll showed 71 per cent think it should be the norm. In 2021, less than

10 per cent of schools were integrated and only 7 per cent of young people attended them.[27] But integrated schools and colleges can shine out. Claire Bailey, a Member of the Legislative Assembly of Northern Ireland, was a pupil in its first year at the pioneering integrated Lagan College. She remembers the hard political context of the 1981 hunger strikes. But the College encouraged a very different conversation.[28] *I remember Brian Lambkin, the RE* [Religious Education] *teacher. With hindsight you realize how special he was as a teacher, he was very, very open. He would bring things into the class and allow people to discuss amongst them … We were going to celebrate all the cultures.* Each child went home to make something for Passover. Claire was to make unleavened bread. *I didn't even know what unleavened bread was. I remember having to go home to my mummy and go, 'I have to make this, I don't know what it is'. And neither did my mum … So that was brought into our home, a bit of learning … And then on the Passover day sitting down as a class and eating all the Jewish food on the table.*

She remembers barrier-breaking friendships. *I was going to school with others who lived very affluent lives on the Malone Road … we were all friends together, we were a gang, … Susan lived just off the Antrim Road, Karen lived up in Ballysillan … there was Joanne who lives in Lisburn, and there was us who lived in Antrim and Louise who lived up the Malone Road. But we all stayed together. We all slept in each other's houses … I was integrated into … so many different communities and cultures …. I walked these streets and had friends living in them all … I never had a sense of exclusion from any part of the city … I loved that I went to Lagan. Lagan still pulls strings in my heart. I wouldn't have missed a day.*

The case against segregated education has several thrusts. Segregated schools can fail to challenge hostilities. Schooling can be inferior for the less powerful group. Segregated children are deprived of a valuable range of friendships. Mental growth is boosted by a varied intellectual diet. Aren't these points enough? So, should religious schools be banned? But religious freedom is not trivial. Banning schools whose teaching emphasizes one religion seems far too few steps away from the Chinese government's 're-education camps' for Muslims. Children lose from the narrowness of religious segregation, but parental choice about children's development matters.

The case for integrated schools and the case for religious freedom are each strong. But there are ways of coming closer to having both. Religious groups should be free to set up their own schools. Restrictions on what they do teach should come from banning incitement to violence or hatred. But omissions matter too. There is a need to protect children from major deprivation. They are harmed if their religious education stops them learning to read, or denies them mathematics, science, history, literature, languages, art or music. Subject to that, religious schools should of course be free to teach their beliefs and practices. But total segregation is unnecessary. 'No friends outside our religion' or 'no discussions with those who are not with us'. Isn't such a restricted emotional and intellectual diet another deprivation?[29] Freedom to teach a religion can go with substantial integration. In Berlin, the House of One has a synagogue, a mosque and a church, linked by a shared communal room. Why not have schools where Muslims and Jews separate for religious instruction and worship, but play together, talk together, eat together (with their different diets) and learn science, literature, art, music, computing, languages, history and mathematics together? (This thought supports encouraging, not enforcing, such projects.) On a *very* optimistic version, even more benefit would come if discussions included why people have different beliefs, how to discuss them across the divide, and how to think about what is true.)

Israel–Palestine: Integrated Schools and the Possibility of Peace

Asaf Ronel, an editor of *Haaretz* and father of a child at an integrated school in Jaffa, is clear about the benefits of integration. There is an obvious difference between rarely meeting children on the other side and going to school with them every day. There they can start to understand the others' history without diminishing their own.

Ethnic Arabs are about 20 per cent of Israel's citizens. Israeli–Palestinian integrated schools do exist. In 1997, two years after Rabin's assassination, the Jewish-Israeli Lee Gordon and the Palestinian-Israeli Amin Khalaf planned their integrated school, Hand in Hand. It started with 55 students. In 2019 Hand in Hand was the largest integrated network, with two thousand students in six schools and over a thousand on the waiting list. In younger classes, Arab and Jewish children sit alternately. Later this is unnecessary. There are sessions where parents are encouraged to tell their family's stories. Nadia, an Arab-Israeli mother of two children there, was appreciative: *People are connecting over pain, over sadness. It doesn't matter who. It doesn't matter on what side. All of a sudden, we're together.*[30] When violence flares up, there are discussion meetings for children *and* for parents.

In Jaffa there is a rare Palestinian–Jewish couple, Ora Balha and her husband Ihab. He takes the children to the Mosque for Friday prayers. Then the family is together for Shabbat. When they first looked, there was no integrated kindergarten. They opened one, celebrating the children's Jewish, Muslim and Christian cultures and languages. In 2016 it had sixty-five children. In 2013 there was a second integrated kindergarten opened by Hand in Hand. Violence sometimes intrudes on integrated schools. In 2014, *Death to Arabs* was spray-painted on the Hand in Hand school in Jerusalem. The school community responded with a soft voice. They put up a banner: *There is cooperation, love and friendship here between Arabs and Jews.* Three weeks later arsonists burned down a classroom and scrawled *There is no coexistence with cancer.* One sign of hope: the students stayed united in support of the school. It is sad the arsonists had been so much less lucky in their education.

IV: Two Projects

People vary in how far they move from the biased group narrative towards self-creation. What could help? Two brief thoughts about conversations: one about film-making, one about poetry.

Rival Narrators in Conversation: A Film Project

This needs two teams of film-makers, one Palestinian and one Israeli. Each would make a film, from their own side's perspective, about a slice of the conflict's history. They would use news film and have technical support. They could interview victims from their own side and others who remember the events.

While writing *The Principles of Psychology*, William James wrote to his brother Henry: '*I have to forge every sentence in the teeth of irreducible and stubborn facts*'.[31] Each team, before presenting their story as powerfully as they could, would be reminded to respect unwelcome facts. It is no good telling victims these things did not happen. Peace must be forged in the teeth of these irreducible and stubborn facts. Subject to this, each story would display their own side's memories, hopes, bitterness or fear.

The two groups would meet to see and discuss their films. (Underneath an uncaptioned duck-rabbit picture?) A start with shared problems, such as finding articulate witnesses, passionate, but not fanatical or hysterical. Then divisive problems about truth and objectivity. This would need supportive chairing, willing to probe *and* to extend sympathy to each side. What evidence suggests a reliable witness? Where the films disagree, is it likely that either has the whole truth? How close to the irreducible and stubborn facts are most people's memories? What helps get closer? Could there be a film that would do justice to the humanly important truths in each of theirs? The final request: go away as one group and try to make the film a modern Tolstoy might make. (Impossible, of course. But worth keeping in mind.) Perhaps invite both former Shin Bet leaders hoping to escape the cycle of violence and imprisoned senior men from Hamas or Islamic Jihad who have expressed repentance in Israeli prison. The hope would be to stimulate many more than the two film teams. Their working together would also be filmed, to be shown widely with their final joint film.

The project could fail in so many ways. It would be unfair if one team was sympathetic, intelligent and open-minded, while the other was bad-tempered, stupid and dogmatic. Even balanced teams could become too angry. Or those chairing the discussions could be unintelligent or biased. Despite the risks, a project along these lines (in improved versions correcting early errors?) may be worth trying. It would be a conversation, partly verbal, partly more, that just might weaken the grip of denial and bitterness.

Sounds of Self-Creation: The Voice of Poetry in the Conversation of Mankind

I like Michael Oakeshott's words: *Poetry is a sort of truancy, a dream within the dream of life, a wild flower planted among our wheat.*[32] It crops up in surprising places. Bin Laden's 9/11 attack on New York made him one of history's most appalling mass murderers. But even mass murderers may need poetry. In a letter written shortly before 9/11 he wanted a leader for a big operation inside America. In the next sentence, he asked: *If there are any brothers with you who know about poetic meters, please inform me, and if you have any books on classical prosody, please send them to me.*[33]

Writing poems does not begin to excuse his mass-murdering attack on New York. Poetry often plays a role in the lives of jihadis, sometimes – despite the violent outlook – a self-creative one. Group poetry readings usually have strong political content. Poems are often dark, vilifying Shias, Jews and the West. But sometimes sympathy with Muslim victims is expressed without hatred of enemies. As Robyn Cresswell and Bernard Haykel explain, *Jihadi poems are best understood not as works of propaganda or recreation, but as performances of authenticity. The poets are ... telling each other who they are, or at least how they would like to be seen. This work of self-fashioning is a cultural task as much as it is a political one.*[34] Poetry in the Arab world is hugely popular. An Abu Dhabi television programme of people reciting their own poetry has an audience of ten million.

Listening For the Sounds of Self-Creation

Kate Clanchy, a poet at Oxford Spires Academy, described a moment in her teaching: *'Is it a good poem?' asks Heya.*

'Yes', I say. 'I will tell him it is a good poem', says Heya. And
she does, in Arabic, and he smiles. 'Tell him', I say, 'that he
has a very grown-up poet living inside him'. She does and
this makes them both laugh. Then I say, 'Tell him, please,
that if you are a poet it is hard to lose your language, very,
very hard. But he can get it back ... He can learn to write in
English too' ... And I thought, not for the first time, it is me,
not the children, learning the lessons here ... So many of the
children had a loss to mourn, a country, a family, – and in
the end, isn't that what poetry is for? By the rivers of Babylon
we sat down and wept.*[35]*

Shukria Rezaei was a refugee from Afghanistan. Kate
Clanchy encouraged her to write poetry. Here is part of a
poem she wrote at the age of eighteen:

> I haven't touched your grenades or your bullets:
> nor worn your chain of bullets around my neck
> and claimed jihad;
> but I have touched broken lives,
> shattered glass,
> and walked on an injured land,
> where blood oozes and boils
> until the steam reaches your nostrils.
>
> I haven't read the Quran you have read
> where to kill is fine
> where rape is acceptable.
> But I have read the Quran of Prophet Mohammad (PBUH)
> where killing one person is killing all of humanity.*[36]*

From SHUKRIA REZAEI: *To the Taliban.*

Integrated Israeli–Palestinian education is important for
peace-making. But being together at school is not the
whole story. It matters which topics students take up in
the conversation of mankind. Conversations need not be
about who is in the right, or which religion is true. Perhaps
gentle coaxing to talk about things that express who they
are? (Here, teachers' feel for their personal chemistry with
a student will be crucial in deciding whether or when to
try.) Responses to experiences should be heard. Writing
their own poems – and listening to each other's – would
not be a bad start. Students' first responses may be about

football, music or clothes. If they make their own music or write their own poems, they may be shy about it. Friendship across barriers may be easier if they can be helped over the shyness.

EPILOGUE

Leaders playing their competitive games can be unmoved by horrendous human costs, as in Putin's attack on Ukraine. At their different stages of the German and French cycle, Bismarck and Clemenceau were each fixated on their two countries' relative power. Neither could see their countries' rivalry would contribute to world wars, in one of which nuclear weapons would be invented and used.

Some leaders may care less about *ending* the Israel–Palestine conflict than about *winning* a current round. This shallowness can seem eternal. Fernand Braudel described Philip II of Spain attending, not to the deep currents of his age, but to dramatic topical events. Braudel called them *brief, rapid, nervous fluctuations … surface disturbances, crests of foam that the tides of history carry on their strong backs. So, the historian who takes a seat in Philip II's chair and reads his papers finds himself transported into a strange one-dimensional world, a world of strong passions certainly, blind like any other living world, our own included, and unconscious of the deeper realities of history, of the running waters on which our frail barks are tossed like cockleshells.*[1]

Crises leave little time for the deep tides of history. It is harsh to blame leaders for their one-dimensional world. But the rest of us can ask the ignored questions. On the diagnosis suggested here, we are often trapped in our conflicts by psychological fault lines that shape them. It would help to talk less about who first provoked or humiliated the other side, and instead talk with them about how to weaken the grip of fault lines we share. Backlash, rigid belief systems, identity distortions all go so deep. But, if we look, we can see they are traps. Future generations may find our thinking about them too simple. Still, perhaps we should take up the clues we do have about escaping them.

NOTES

Notes in bold type add details or commentary to a point in the text.

Prologue

Chapter 1: Disputed Homeland

1 Psalm 137, verses 1–4.
2 Mourid Barghouti: *I Saw Ramallah*, translated by Ahdaf Soueif, London: Bloomsbury, 2004, pp. 6–7.
3 Ghada Karmi: *In Search of Fatima, A Palestinian Story*, London: Verso Books, 2002, pp. 125 and 123.
4 Barghouti, pp. 35–6.
5 Amos Oz: *A Tale of Love and Darkness*, translated by Nicholas de Lange, London: Houghton Mifflin Harcourt, 2004, pp. 345–6.
6 David Grossman: Confronting the Beast, *Guardian*, 15 September 2007.
7 Shlomo Sand: *The Invention of the Jewish People*, translated by Yael Lotan, London: Verso, 2009, pp. 129 and 149.
8 Benedict Anderson: *Imagined Communities, Reflections on the Origins and Spread of Nationalism*, London: Verso, 1983; Ernest Gellner: *Nations and Nationalism*, Oxford: Blackwell,

1983; Eric Hobsbawm: *Nations and Nationalism Since 1780: Programme, Myth, Reality*, Cambridge: Cambridge University Press, 1990; Basil Davidson: *The Black Man's Burden: Africa and the Curse of the Nation-state*, Oxford: James Currey, 1992; Linda Colley: *Britons: Forging the Nation 1707–1837*, London: Yale University Press, 1992; Eric Hobsbawm and Terence Ranger (eds.): *The Invention of Tradition*, Cambridge: Cambridge University Press, 1996; Raphael Samuel: *Theatres of Memory*, vol. II, *Island Stories, Unravelling Britain*, London: Verso, 1998.

9   Gellner, chapter 3.

10 Anderson, p. 15.

11 Herodotus: *The Histories*, translated by Tom Holland, with an Introduction by Paul Cartledge, London: Penguin, 2013, Book 8, p. 144.

12 Theodor Herzl, quoted in Shlomo Avineri: *Theodor Herzl and the Foundation of the Jewish State*, London: Phoenix, 2008, pp. 160–1.

13 Theodor Herzl: *Tagebücher, 1*, pp. 33 and 269–70, quoted in Carl E. Schorske: *Fin-de-Siecle Vienna, Politics and Culture*, New York: Vintage Books, 1981, p. 165.

14 *Guardian*, 25 September 2015.

15 Victor Klemperer: *I Shall Bear Witness*, translated by Martin Chalmers, London: Phoenix, pp. 161, 390, 397, 410–11, 412 and 414.

16 Theodor Herzl: *The Jewish State* (originally *Der Judenstadt* [Vienna, 1896]), translated by Sylvie d'Avigdor, London: Penguin, 2010, pp. 8–9.

17 *Sunday Times*, July 1969.

18 Ilan Pappé: *The Ethnic Cleansing of Palestine*, London: One World, 2007, p. 277, quoting Dan Kurzman: *Soldier of Peace*, pp. 140–1.

19 Mahmoud Darwish: The Homeland between Memory and History, in *Journal of an Ordinary Grief*, translated by Ibrahim Muhawi, New York: Archipelago Books, 2010, p. 38.

20 The Balfour Declaration is rightly taken to have promised a Jewish state in Palestine, despite a reservation about not prejudicing the rights of existing non-Jewish communities: *His Majesty's Government view with favour the establishment in Palestine of a national home for the Jewish people and will use their best endeavours to facilitate the achievement of this object …* The British government also made a promise to the Arabs that was incompatible with this, in letters from

Sir Henry McMahon to Sharif (later King) Hussein: Great Britain is prepared to recognize and support the independence within the territories included within the limits and boundaries proposed by the Sharif of Mecca (Letter, 24 October 1915). The Foreign Secretary at the time, Sir Edward Grey, in his memoirs, referred to *the promise to King Hussein that Arabia should be an entirely independent Moslem state.* Lord Grey of Falloden*: Twenty-five Years, 1892–1916*, London: Hodder and Stoughton, 1925, vol. 1, p. 229. T.E. Lawrence, fighting with the Arab rebellion against Germany's ally Turkey, was clear about deceiving the Arabs: *The Arab revolt had begun on false pretences ... I could see that if we won the war the promises to the Arabs were dead paper ... Yet the Arab inspiration was our main tool in winning the Eastern War. So I assured them that England kept her word in letter and in spirit ... instead of being proud of what we did together, I was continually and bitterly ashamed.* T.E. Lawrence: *Seven Pillars of Wisdom, a Triumph,* privately printed, London, 1926, London: Penguin, 1962 and 2000, pp. 22–3.

21 Balfour's claim and Khalidi's response both in Rashid Khalidi: *Palestinian Identity, The Construction of Modern National Consciousness*, New York: Columbia University Press, 1997, p. 252, note 9.

22 Yusuf al-Din al-Khalidi, quoted in Nur Masalha: *Palestine, a Four Thousand Year History*, London: Zed Books, 2018, chapter 9, pp. 284–5.

23 Raja Shehadeh: *Palestinian Walks, Notes on a Vanishing Landscape*, London: Profile Books, 2007 and 2008, p. 22.

24 Ibid., p. 15.

25 Ibid., p. 17.

26 Tony Judt: Fictions on the Ground, in Jennifer Homans (ed.): *Tony Judt: When the Facts Change, Essays 1995–2010*, London: Penguin, Random House, pp. 142–6.

27 The Owl's Night, translated by Amira el-Zein, in Mahmoud Darwish: *Unfortunately, it was Paradise: Selected Poems*, Berkeley: University of California Press, 2003, p. 64.

28 Mahmoud Darwish was told this by an Israeli who took part. Mahmoud Darwish: The Moon Did Not Fall into the Well, in *Journal of an Ordinary Grief*, p. 13.

29 Ibid., p. 21.

30 Mahmoud Darwish: *Palestine as Metaphor*, translated by Amira el-Zein and Carolyn Forché, Northampton, MA: Olive Branch Press, 2019, pp. 54 and 61.

31 Mahmoud Darwish: I Belong There, translated by Caroline Forché, in Darwish: *Unfortunately, it was Paradise.*

Chapter 2: Wounds and Backlash

1 Johann Gottlieb Fichte: *Addresses to the German Nation* [1808], translated by Isaac Nakhimovsky, Bella Kapossy and Keith Tribe, Indianapolis, IN: Hackett, 2013, pp. 176–8.

2 Michael Howard: *The Franco-Prussian War: The German Invasion of France, 1870–1871*, 2nd edn, London: Routledge, 2001. The quoted comment was echoing and supporting Gerhard Rittler: *Staatskunst und Kriegshandwerk: das Problem des Militarismus in Deutschland*, vol. 1, Munich, 1954.

3 Howard, pp. 40–76.

4 Both quoted in Robert Jervis: *Perception and Misperception in International Politics*, new edn, Princeton, NJ: Princeton University Press, 2017, pp. 98–9.

5 Joseph Reinach: *Dépêches, Circulaires, Décrets, Proclamations, et Discours de Leon Gambetta, Paris, 1986*, vol. 1, pp. 197–212, quoted in Howard, pp. 388–9.

6 Moritz Busch: *Bismarck: Some Secret Pages of his History*, London 1898, vol. 1, quoted in Howard, p. 395.

7 Karl Marx and Friedrich Engels: *Collected Works*, New York: International Publishers, 1976, vol. 44, p. 120, quoted in Tristram Hunt: *The Frock-Coated Communist, The Life and Times of the Original Champagne Socialist*, London: Penguin, 2010, p. 251.

8 John Maynard Keynes: Dr Melchior: A Defeated Enemy, in *Two Memoirs*, London: Rupert Hart-Davis, 1949.

9 Harold Nicolson: *Peacemaking, 1919*, London: Faber and Faber, 1933, p. 43.

10 John Maynard Keynes: *The Economic Consequences of the Peace*, London: Macmillan, 1920, pp. 29–33. Keynes's pen portraits of participants attracted much controversy, discussed in Robert Skidelsky: *John Maynard Keynes: Hopes Betrayed, 1883–1920*, London: Macmillan, 1983, pp. 392–400. Skidelsky's adjudication is that Keynes got Wilson 'more wrong than right', but that he 'got Clemenceau about right'. Margaret Macmillan is not a fan of Keynes ('A very clever, rather ugly young man … His membership of the Bloomsbury circle only enhanced his propensity to moral superiority'). She rightly gives space also to Clemenceau's view of Wilson and Lloyd George: *I find myself between Jesus Christ on the one hand and Napoleon Bonaparte*

on the other. He saw Lloyd George as *wriggling out of agreements.* His version of Wilson was a bit like Keynes's: *What ignorance of Europe and how difficult all understandings were with him! He believed you could do everything by formulas and his fourteen points. God himself was content with ten commandments. Wilson modestly inflicted fourteen points on us ... the fourteen commandments of the most empty theory!* (Quoted in Margaret Macmillan: *Paris, 1919, Six Months that Changed the World,* London: John Murray, 2019, pp. 40–1 and 192.

A very different character from Keynes, T.E. Lawrence, for different reasons, agreed with his negative view of what these old men achieved: *We lived many lives in these whirling campaigns, never sparing ourselves; yet when we achieved and the new world dawned, the old men came out again and took our victory to re-make in the likeness of the former world they knew. Youth could win, but had not learned to keep: and was pitiably weak as against age. We stammered that we had worked for a new heaven and a new earth, and they thanked us kindly and made their peace.* T.E. Lawrence: *Seven Pillars of Wisdom, a Triumph,* privately printed, 1926, London: Penguin, 1962 and 2000, pp. 22–3.

11 Macmillan, p. 36.
12 William Shirer: *Berlin Diary, 1934–1941,* New York: Alfred A. Knopf, 1941, pp. 328–32.
13 Jonathan Freedland, *Guardian,* 5 July 2014.
14 David Shulman, *Dark Hope, Working for Peace in Israel and Palestine,* Chicago, IL: University of Chicago Press, 2007, pp. 50–2.
15 In this paragraph the account and quotes come from Oliver Holmes: Scores left homeless as Israeli forces raze Palestinian village, *Guardian,* 6 November 2020.
16 Jerusalem Center for Public Affairs: *Jerusalem Letter,* 3 January 2002.
17 Kanan Makiya: *Cruelty and Silence,* London: Jonathan Cape, 1993, p. 285.
18 The friend is Jeff McMahan, White's Professor of Moral Philosophy at Oxford.
19 Gilbert Achcar: *Les Arabes et la Shoah,* Paris: Actes Sud; English translation by G.M. Goshgarian: *The Arabs and the Holocaust, the Arab–Israeli War of Narratives,* London: Saqi Books, 2010, p. 270.
20 Mahmoud Abbas: *The Other Side: The Secret Relationship between Nazism and Zionism,* published in Arabic 1984. For

an account of the book, see Edy Cohen: How Holocaust Denial Shaped Mahmoud Abbas' World View, *The Tower*, May 2016.

21 Mahmoud Abbas apologises for holocaust speech, *Guardian*, 4 May 2018.

22 Anne Marie Oliver and Paul Steinberg: *The Road to Martyrs' Square, A Journey into the World of the Suicide Bomber*, New York: Oxford University Press, 2005, p. 63.

23 Nonie Darwish: Raised for Jihad: A Shahid's Daughter Speaks Out, in Judy Kuriansky (ed.): *Terror in the Holy Land, Inside the Anguish of the Israeli–Palestinian Conflict*, Westport, CT: Praeger, 2006, pp. 27–8.

24 Ibid., pp. 27 and 30.

25 Human Rights Watch: *Jenin: IDF Military Operations*, published online, May 2002.

26 Any serious discussion of the cycle of violence has to consider particular episodes where disputing witnesses make certainty unobtainable. Historians, like juries in some court cases, and sometimes the rest of us, often have to make judgements about relative degrees of plausibility. These uncertainties apply not only to particular events, as at Jenin, but also to broad-brush portraits of longer periods, as in this book. As a non-historian who lives far from Israel–Palestine, I am very conscious of these limitations. But I am a bit cheered by the great Dutch historian Pieter Geyl, who wrote: *the analysis of so many conflicting opinions concerning one historical phenomenon is not just a means of whiling away the time, nor need it lead to discouraging conclusions concerning the untrustworthiness of historical study. The study even of contradictory conceptions can be fruitful. Any one thesis or presentation may in itself be unacceptable, and yet, when it has been jettisoned, there remains something of value. Its very critics are that much richer. History is indeed an argument without end.* Pieter Geyl: *Napoleon, For and Against*, London: Jonathan Cape, 1949, and London: Penguin, 1965, p. 18.

27 BBC News website, 22 April 2002.

28 Human Rights Watch, 2002.

29 How Jenin Battle became a 'Massacre', *Guardian*, 6 May 2002.

30 Human Rights Watch: *Jenin: IDF Military Operations*, 2002, Part VII.

31 Barbara Victor: *Army of Roses, Inside the World of Palestine Women Suicide Bombers*. Rodale Publishers, 2003, p. 189.

32 Scott Atran: *Talking to the Enemy, Violent Extremism, Sacred Values and What it Means to be Human*, London: Allen Lane, 2010, p. 360.

33 Edward S. Herman and Noam Chomsky: *Manufacturing Consent, The Political Economy of the Mass Media*, New York: Pantheon, 1988; London: Vintage, 1994.

34 Daniel Dor: *The Suppression of Guilt, The Israeli Media and the Reoccupation of the West Bank*, London: Pluto Press, 2005.

35 Ibid., p. 6.

36 Sone reviews of Dor's book: Daphna Baram, *Guardian*, 7 November 2005; Mike Berry: *Holy Land Studies*, 2006; Jan Voelkel: *Arab Media and Society*, 1 March 2007.

37 Breaking the Silence: *Our Harsh Logic, Israeli Soldiers' Testimonies from the Occupied Territories, 2000–2010*, New York: Picador, 2013.

38 Ibid., pp. 18–19.

39 Ibid., p. 39.

40 Ibid., p. 186.

41 Ibid., pp. 19–20.

42 *The Book of Judges*, chapter 16.

43 John Milton: *Samson Agonistes*, 1671, lines 38–42 and 53–4.

44 Hitler: *Mein Kampf*, translated by Ralph Manheim, London: Pimlico, 1992, p. 279.

45 Raul Hilberg: *The Destruction of the European Jews*, London: Holmes and Meier, 1985, p. 233.

46 *The Goebbels Diaries*, translated and edited by Louis P. Lochner, London: Hamish Hamilton, 1948, pp. 296–7.

47 Beverley Milton-Edwards and Stephen Farrell: *Hamas*, Cambridge: Polity Press, 2010, p. 15.

48 Amira Hass: *Drinking the Sea at Gaza, Days and Nights in a Land under Siege*, New York: Henry Holt and Co., 1996, p. 124.

49 Then Deputy Prime Minister, Ehud Olmert, quoted in Henry Gordis: *Israel-Gaza Conflict, What Everyone Needs to Know*, copyright 2021 Henry Gordis, pp. 63–4.

50 Quoted in Gordis, pp. 66–7.

51 Milton-Edwards and Farrell, p. 298.

52 Avi Shlaim, *Guardian*, 7 January 2019.

53 Norman G. Finkelstein: *Gaza, An Inquest into its Martyrdom*, Oakland, CA: University of California Press, 2018, pp. 137–56.

54 Sara Roy: *Failing Peace, Gaza and the Palestinian Conflict*, London: Pluto Press, 2007, p. 33.

55 Amira Hass: *Drinking the Sea at Gaza, Days and Nights in a Land under Siege*, translated by Elana Wesley and Maxine Kaufman-Lacusta, New York: Metropolitan Books, 1999; paperback edition: Holt Paperbacks, 2000, p. 143.

56 Statement first posted on the web in 2012, English translation, with an introduction by Avishai Margalit, *New York*

Review of Books, 10 January 2013. Nomika Zion lives in Sderot, sometimes targeted in bombardment from Gaza. Israel's standard retaliation was heavy bombardment. Her statement was written during one retaliation.

57 George Orwell: *Looking Back on the Spanish War*, in Sonia Orwell and Ian Angus (eds.): *The Collected Essays, Journalism and Letters of George Orwell*, vol. 2, *My Country Right or Left*, London: Penguin, 1970, p. 289.

58 Breaking the Silence, p. 315.

59 Dr Eyad Sarraj: Why We Have Become Suicide Bombers, Understanding Terror, *Dossier Palestina August 1997*.

60 Roney Srour: Challenges of a Young Palestinian Clinician during the Second Intifada, in Judy Kuriansky (ed.): *Terror in the Holy Land, Inside the Anguish of the Israeli–Palestinian Conflict*, pp. 199–202.

61 Nasser Abufarha: *The Making of a Human Bomb, an Ethnography of Palestinian Resistance*, Durham, NC: Duke University Press, 2009.

62 Ibid., pp. 9–12.

63 Ibid., p. 23.

64 Ibid., pp. 147–56.

65 Ibid., p. 150.

66 Yonah Dovid Bardos: A Bomb on the Bus, in Kuriansky, p. 50.

67 Abufarha, p. 13.

68 Atran, p. 362.

69 Gideon Aran: *The Smile of the Human Bomb, New Perspectives on Suicide Terrorism*, translated by Jeffrey Green, Ithaca, NY: Cornell University Press, 2018, p. 104.

70 Ibid., p. 106.

71 Ibid., p. 108.

72 Ibid., p. 36.

73 Ibid., p. 41.

74 Here a major source is Dror Moreh, *The Gatekeepers, Inside Israel's Internal Security Agency*, New York: Skyhorse Publishing, 2015, based on Moreh's remarkable 2012 documentary, *The Gatekeepers,* in which former Shin Bet heads answer questions about targeted killing, torture, etc. Probably many intelligence services use these methods. Watching, at times I suspect cover-up, but sometimes I am torn between revulsion at things done and respect for the seriousness and relative openness with which they are discussed. The text of the book is fuller than the English subtitles of the documentary. I draw heavily on both here. I thank George Szmukler for telling me about the documentary.

75 Moreh, p. 41.
76 Ronen Bergman: *Rise and Kill First, The Secret History of Israel's Targeted Assassinations*, London: John Murray, 2018, pp. 539–40.
77 Ibid., p. 542.
78 Ibid., p. 549.
79 Jean Améry: *At the Mind's Limits*, translated by Sidney and Stella P. Rosenfeld, New York: Schocken Books, 1986, pp. 22–8.
80 United Nations Convention against Torture, Article 1.
81 Human Rights Watch: *Two Authorities, One Way, Zero Dissent*.
82 Moreh, p. 77.
83 Human Rights Watch/Middle East: *Torture and Ill-Treatment, Israel's Interrogation of Palestinians from the Occupied Territories*, 1994.
84 Teresa Thornhill: *Making Women Talk, The Interrogation of Palestinian Women Detainees by the Israeli General Security Services*, London: Lawyers for Palestinian Rights, 1992, p. 27.
85 I quote Israeli versions of these euphemisms. I have no equivalent Palestinian examples, but it is hard to believe there are none. So I feel free to contrast them with the realities of interrogation on both sides.
86 Ya'akov Peri, in Moreh, p. 117.

Chapter 3: Breaking the Cycle?

1 Quoted by the Israeli psychologist and therapist Ofra Ayalon.
2 Davud Kaposi: *Violence and Understanding in Gaza, The British Broadsheets' Coverage of the War*, London: Palgrave Macmillan, 2014, p. 183.
3 Ya'akov Peri, in Moreh, pp. 587–8.
4 Moreh, pp. 250–1.
5 Atran, p. 367.
6 Shulman, pp. 180–1.
7 Srour, in Kuriansky, pp. 197–8.
8 Avraham Rivkind: Awaiting the Wounded: A Doctor's Story, in Kuriansky, p. 195.
9 Quoted in Anthony Kenny: *The Road to Hillsborough*, Oxford: Pergamon Press, 1986, p. 68.
10 Quoted in Kenny, pp. 68–9.
11 Mahmoud Darwish: *A Rhyme for the Odes* (MU' ALLAQAT), translated by Munir Akash and Carolyn Forché in their selection of Darwish's poems: *Unfortunately, it was Paradise*.

MU' ALLAQAT refers to a collection of seven odes by classic sixth-century Arab poets. Darwish hoped his poem, written in such different times would 'rhyme' with theirs.

12 Uri Savir: *The Process, 1,100 Days that Changed the Middle East,* New York: Vintage Books: 1998, p. 83.

13 Ahmed Qurie: *From Oslo to Jerusalem, The Palestinian Story of the Secret Negotiations*, New York: I.B. Tauris, 2006, p. 40.

14 Ibid., p. 148.

15 Ibid., p. 151.

16 Savir, p. 61.

17 Ibid., p. 28.

18 Ya'akov Peri, in Moreh, p. 108.

19 Ibid.

20 Qurie, p. 145.

21 Savir, pp. 31–2.

22 Ibid., pp. 207–8.

23 Ibid., pp. 115–16.

24 Qurie, pp. 212–13.

25 Savir, pp. 46–7.

26 Ibid., p. 47.

27 John Rawls: *A Theory of Justice*, Cambridge, MA: Harvard University Press, 1970.

28 Edward W. Said: *The End of the Peace Process, Oslo and After*, New York: Vintage, 2001, p. 15.

29 Qurie, p. 297.

30 Savir, p. 312.

31 Raja Shehadeh: *When the Birds Stopped Singing, Life in Ramallah under Siege*, Hanover, NH: Steerforth Press, 2003, p. 142.

32 In the newspaper *Yedioth Ahronoth*, quoted in Dan Ephron: *Killing a King. The Assassination of Yitzhak Rabin and the Remaking of Israel*, New York: W.W. Norton, 2015, p. 32.

33 Savir, p. 34.

34 Qurie, p. 11.

35 Ephron, p. 72.

36 Moreh, p. 162.

37 Ibid., p. 160.

38 Poll in Yedioth Ahronoth, quoted in Ephron, p. 78.

39 Moreh, p. 181.

40 Robert Axelrod: *The Evolution of Cooperation*, New York: Basic Books, 1984, republished London: Penguin Books, 1990.

41 William Ian Miller: *Bloodtaking and Peacemaking, Feud, Law, and Society in Saga Iceland*, Chicago, IL: University of Chicago Press, 1990, p. 374.

42 Bernard Wasserstein: *Israelis and Palestinians, Why do they Fight? Can they stop?*, 3rd edn New Haven, CT: Yale University Press, 2008, pp. 91–3.

43 Amira Hass: *Drinking the Sea at Gaza, Days and Nights in a Land under Siege*, translated by Elana Wesley and Maxine Kaufman-Lacusta, New York: Henry Holt and Company, 2000; Friends of the Earth Middle East: *Why Cooperate over Water? Shared Waters of Palestine, Israel and Jordan: Cross-border Crises and the Need for Trans-national Solutions*, Amman, Bethlehem and Tel Aviv, 2010.

44 Quoted in Ilan Pappé: *The Ethnic Cleansing of Palestine*, London: One World, 2006, p. 48.

45 Simcha Flapan: *The Birth of Israel: Myths and Realities*, New York: Pantheon Books, 1987, p. 17.

46 Benny Morris: *One State, Two States, Resolving the Israel–Palestine Conflict*, New Haven, CT: Yale University Press, 2009, p. 169.

47 Amos Oz: Between Right and Right, in *Help Us to Divorce*, London: Vintage, 2004, pp. 39–40.

48 Uri Avnery: *Israel without Zionism, A Plan for Peace in the Middle East*, New York: Collier Books, 1971, p. 238. (Originally published 1968.)

49 Omar Dahbour: Self-Determination and Power-Sharing in Israel/Palestine, *Ethnopolitics*, 15:4, 2016, p. 397.

Chapter 4: Joining the Conversation of Mankind

1 Michael Oakeshott: The Voice of Poetry in the Conversation of Mankind, in his *Rationalism in Politics and Other Essays*, 2nd edn, Carmel, IN: Liberty Fund, 1991, pp. 488–541.

2 Daniel Barenboim and Edward Said: *Parallels and Paradoxes, Explorations in Music and Society*, edited with a preface by Ara Guzelimian, London: Bloomsbury, 2003, pp. 166–8.

3 Shulman, pp. 154–5.

4 Leading UK Jewish figures condemn Israel's West Bank plans, *Guardian*, 6 June 2020.

5 Moreh, p. 237.

6 Maxine Kaufman-Lacusta: *Refusing to be Enemies, Palestinian and Israeli Resistance to the Occupation*, Reading: Ithaca Press, 2011, p. 11.

7 Quotes in this account of Budrus not attributed to other sources

come from the brilliant documentary created by Just Vision and directed by Julia Bacha.

8 Quote from interview in Ida Audeh: A Village Mobilized: Lessons from Budrus, *The Electronic Intifada*, 13 June 2007.

9 Sari Nusseibeh: *What is a Palestinian State Worth?* Cambridge, MA: Harvard University Press, 2011, p. 202.

10 Rabbi Arik Ascherman, quoted in Kaufman-Lacusta, p. 160.

11 Amos Oz: Between Right and Right, pp. 8–9.

Chapter 5: The Psychology of Backlash

1 J.M. Wallace-Hadrill: The Bloodfeud of the Franks, in *The Long-haired Kings, and Other Studies in Frankish History*, London: Methuen, 1962. (Quote from the re-published edition, London: Routledge, 2020, p. 124.)

2 **William Ian Miller: *Bloodtaking and Peacemaking, Feud, Law and Society in Saga Iceland*, Chicago, IL: University of Chicago Press, 1990, pp. 184–5. I have drawn heavily on this wide-ranging and stimulating book.**

3 Wallace-Hadrill, p. 129.

4 E.E. Evans-Pritchard: *The Nuer, A Description of the Modes of Livelihood and Political Institutions of a Nilotic People*, Oxford: The Clarendon Press, 1940, p. 151.

5 Christopher Boehm: *Blood Revenge, The Enactment and Management of Conflict in Montenegro and other Tribal Societies*, Lawrence, KS: University of Kansas Press, 1984, p. 65.

6 Keith M. Brown: *Bloodfeud in Scotland, 1573–1625: Violence, Justice and Politics in an Early Modern Society*, Edinburgh: John Donald, 1986, p. 29, quoted in John Lindow: Bloodfeud and Scandinavian Mythology, *alvissmal* 4, 1994, p. 60.

7 Evans-Pritchard, pp. 161, 163–4, 173–6.

8 Boehm, chapter 7.

9 Evans-Prichard, pp. 154–5.

10 Wallace-Hadrill, p. 143.

11 Mahmoud Darwish: *Journal of an Ordinary Grief*, p. 20.

12 Avishai Margalit: *The Decent Society*, Cambridge, MA: Harvard University Press, 1996, p. 1.

13 Michael Rosen: *Dignity, Its History and Meaning*, Cambridge, MA: Harvard University Press, 2012, p. 127.

14 Sari Nusseibeh: *Once Upon a Country, a Palestinian Life*, New York: Farrar, Straus and Giroux, 2007, p. 311.

Chapter 6: The Illusions of Backlash

1 Catherine Dawson, letter to the *Guardian*, November 2001.
2 David Shulman: *Dark Hope, Working for Peace in Israel and Palestine*, Chicago, IL: University of Chicago Press, 2007, p. 87.
3 Atran, p. 358.
4 Martha Nussbaum, *Anger and Forgiveness – Resentment, Generosity, Justice*, Oxford: Oxford University Press, 2016, p. 178.
5 Victor, pp. 236–7.
6 This is not just one Palestinian's view. A Hamas student leader says, 'We fight with any means. They have tanks, planes and atom bombs. We have "human bombs". When they stop killing us, we will stop killing them.' Atran, p. 365.
7 Miller, p. 186.

Chapter 7: Collective Guilt: The Role of Stereotypes

1 Mohammad Sidique Khan: Statement aimed at justifying his terrorist bomb at Edgware Station on the London underground, 2005.
2 Ali Fayyad: We are defending our sovereignty; Isaac Herzog: This is a fight for our survival; *Guardian*, 25 July 2006.
3 Quoted in David Grossman: *Sleeping on a Wire, Conversations with Palestinians in Israel*, London: Vintage Books, 2010, p. 287.
4 David H. Hubel: *Eye, Brain, and Vision*, New York: Scientific American Library, 1988, p. 123.
5 David Marr: *Vision*, San Francisco, CA: W.H. Freeman and Company, 1982, reissued 2010, p. 259.
6 Semir Zeki: *Inner Vision, an Exploration of Art and the Brain*, Oxford: Oxford University Press, 1999, pp. 188–9.
7 Donald D. Hoffman: *Visual Intelligence, How We Construct What We See*, New York: W.W. Norton, 2000, p. 114.
8 Richard Gregory: *Eye and Brain, The Psychology of Seeing*, 5th edn, Princeton, NJ: Princeton University Press, 2015; David H. Hubel: *Eye, Brain and Vision*, New York: Scientific American Library, 1988. Some classic papers are in David H. Hubel and Torsten Wiesel: *Brain and Visual Perception, The Story of a 25-year Collaboration*, Oxford: Oxford University Press,

2005. Kant's revolution, replacing passive perception by an active mind imposing its concepts and interpretations on what is perceived, is supported by neuroscience. But neuroscience has not followed Kant's particular model of how this happens. Semir Zeki made the point that Kant's sharp distinction between 'two Faculties, the passive one of Sensibility concerned with the collection of raw sense data and the active one of Understanding which made sense of the raw data' has been undermined. There are many interacting cerebral processes, including re-entry, in which 'the output from a cell, or a group of cells, to another group' is 'reciprocated by a return output from the latter to the former'. Semir Zeki: *A Vision of the Brain*, Oxford: Blackwell, 1993, pp. 143ff and 323. Richard Gregory first used the very influential phrase 'perceptual hypotheses' in a paper he wrote as a Cambridge undergraduate in 1949–50: Brain Function in Terms of Probability and Induction, reprinted in R.L. Gregory: *Concepts and Mechanisms of Perception*, London: Duckworth, 1974, pp. 521–36. Gregory quoted Hermann von Helmholtz as a precursor.

9 E.H. Gombrich: *Art and Illusion, a Study in the Psychology of Pictorial Representation*, London: Phaidon Press, 1960, new edition, 1962, p. 272. Gombrich was aware that his views on Truth and the Stereotype had implications going far beyond art. See the discussion of irrational darkness in Germany in the run-up to Nazism, in his *Aby Warburg, an Intellectual Biography*, 2nd edn, London: Warburg Institute, 1986, p. 321. He quotes Thomas Mann on the exception of Freud, someone who knew the dark side of the psyche but sided with reason. He says the same is true of Warburg. It was true of Gombrich too.

10 Group stereotypes are likely to have different causes from colour recognition, which is probably derived from past successes. The stereotypes are more likely to be transmitted through the culture. Perry Hinton: Implicit Stereotypes and the Predictive Brain, Cognition and Culture in 'Biased' Person Perception, *Palgrave Communications*, 3, 2017.

11 Joseph Jastrow: *Fact and Fable in Psychology*, London: Macmillan, 1901, pp. 294–5.

12 *It may be permissible to speak of the psychic acts of ordinary perception as unconscious conclusions ... Just because they are not free acts of conscious thought, these unconscious conclusions from analogy are irresistible, and the effect of them cannot be overcome by a better understanding of the real relations.* Hermann von Helmholtz: *Treatise on Physiological Optics*, 1910, English translation edited by James P.C. Southall,

Mineola, NY: Dover Books, 1962, reprinted 2005, vol. 3, Part Third: The Theory of the Perception of Vision, section 26: Concerning the Perceptions in General.

13 Victor, p. 158.

14 Ibid., p. 159.

15 The Commission of course did not have a God's eye view. They had a mountain of conflicting testimony, so will sometimes be mistaken. But that limits rather than undermines the great value of their hearings and report. For the problems, see Deborah Posel and Graeme Simpson: The Power of Truth: South Africa's Truth and Reconciliation Commission in Context; Piers Pigou: False Promises and Wasted Opportunities? and The Murder of Sicelo Diomo; and Deborah Posel: The TRC Report: What Kind of History? What Kind of Truth? All in Deborah Posel and Graeme Simpson: *Commissioning the Past, Understanding South Africa's Truth and Reconciliation Commission,* Johannesburg: Witwatersrand University Press, 2002.

16 Report of the Truth and Reconciliation Commission, presented to President Nelson Mandela, October 1998, vol. 1, chapter 5: Concepts and Principles, pp. 103–34.

17 Westphalia Peace Treaties, article 2.

18 Belfast Agreement, 1998, Declaration of Support, paragraphs 2 and 4.

Chapter 8: The Role of Rigid Beliefs

1 This antisemitic reference in Hamas's Constitution does not come from the Quran itself, but from a Hadith (a passage recording an oral tradition attributed to the Prophet). Meir M. Bar-Asher suggests this Hadith is atypical in suggesting that the struggle between Muslims and Jews must be eternal. Meir M. Bar-Asher: *Jews and the Qur'an,* Princeton, NJ: Princeton University Press, 2021, pp. 55–6.

2 Quran, English translation by Talal Itani, 5, 12–13.

3 Quran, Itani translation, 4, 160–1.

4 Genesis, King James translation, 15, 18–21.

5 These two statements are quotes in Idith Zertal and Akiva Eldar: *Lords of the Land, The War over Israel's Settlements in the Occupied Territories, 1967–2007,* translated by Vivian Eden, New York: Nation Books, 2005, pp. 154–5.

6 Gershom Gorenberg: *The End of Days, Fundamentalism and the Struggle for the Temple Mount,* New York: Oxford University Press, 2002, pp. 159, 141 and 239.

7 This comes from Immanuel Kant: *Groundwork of the Metaphysic of Morals*, second section: *Even the Holy One of the Gospels must first be compared with our ideal of moral perfection before we can recognise him as such.*

8 Rebecca Newberger Goldstein: *Betraying Spinoza, The Renegade who Gave us Modernity*, New York: Schocken, 2006, p. 262.

9 Ami Ayalon: *Friendly Fire, How Israel Became its own Worst Enemy and the Hope for its Future*, Lebanon, NH: Steerforth Press, 2020, p. 84.

10 Ibid., p. 83.

11 Ibid., p. 84.

12 Ibid., p. 88.

13 Ibid., p. 89.

14 Ibid., pp. 89–90.

15 Ibid., pp. 90–1.

16 Ibid., p. 93.

17 Ibid., p. 88.

18 *News at Ten*, BBC 1, 12 September 2016.

19 Quoted in Fawaz A. Gerges: *Isis, a History*, Princeton, NJ: Princeton University Press, 2016, p. 40.

20 Jürgen Todenhöfer: *My Journey into the Heart of Terror, Ten Days in the Islamic State*, translated by A.O. May, Vancouver and Berkeley: Greystone Books, 2016.

21 Ibid., p. 60.

22 Ibid., p. 69.

23 Ibid., p. 86.

Chapter 9: Belief Systems: Challenge and Response

1 Daniel Kahneman, Paul Slovic and Amos Tversky (eds.): *Judgment under Uncertainty: Heuristics and Biases*, Cambridge: Cambridge University Press, 1982, especially Parts 1 and 2, cites and discusses many of these local distortions.

2 Francis King and George Matthews (eds.): *About Turn: The British Communist Party and the Second World War: The Verbatim Record of the Central Committee Meeting of 25 September and 2–3 October 1939*, London: Lawrence and Wishart, 1990. The quotations here are taken from pp. 247, 59, 141 and 76. The 'verbatim record' was possible because the whole discussion was bugged. (Twice: once by MI6 and once by Moscow.)

3 Leon Festinger, Henry W. Riecken and Stanley Schachter: *When Prophecy Fails, A Social and Psychological Study of a Modern*

Group that Predicted the Destruction of the World, New York: Harper and Row, 2009.

4 Information here on Rabbi Kook and the later crisis over prophecy is entirely derived from Micah Goodman: *Catch 67: The Left, the Right and the Legacy of the Six-Day War*, New Haven, CT: Yale University Press, 2018, pp. 51–61. Micah Goodman perhaps would disagree with my comments.

5 Ibid., p. 36.

6 Alison Gopnik: *The Philosophical Baby*, London: The Bodley Head, 2009, pp. 10–14.

7 Ludwig Wittgenstein: *On Certainty*, edited by G.E.M. Anscombe and G.H. von Wright, translated by Denis Paul and G.E.M. Anscombe, Oxford: Basil Blackwell, 1969, 1974, paragraphs 83, 103 and 341–3. See also Robert Greenleaf Brice: *Exploring Certainty, Wittgenstein and Wide Fields of Thought*, Plymouth: Lexington Books, 2014, chapters 1 and 2.

8 Wittgenstein, paragraph 108.

9 Allen Buchanan: Social Moral Epistemology, *Social Philosophy and Policy*, 19/2, 2002, 126–52. See also Alvin Goldman: *Knowledge in a Social World*, Oxford: Oxford University Press, 1999.

10 John Berger: *A Fortunate Man*, Harmondsworth: Penguin Books, 1967, p. 102.

11 Edmund Leach: Genesis as Myth, in Leach: *Genesis as Myth and Other Essays*, London: Jonathan Cape, 1969, p. 13.

12 Mary Douglas: *Purity and Danger*, London: Routledge, 1966, p. 67. Page references here are to the 2002 edition.

13 Ibid., p. 37.

14 Ibid., p. 40.

15 John Henry Newman: *Apologia pro Vita Sua*, edited by Ian Ker, London: Penguin, 1994, p. 214.

16 Karl R. Popper: *The Myth of the Framework*, Abingdon, Oxon: Routledge, 1994, pp. 261–75.

17 Otto Neurath: Anti-Spengler, in: *Empiricism and Sociology*, edited by R.S. Cohen and M. Neurath, Dordrecht: Reidel, pp. 312–44.

18 Susan A. Clancy: *Abducted, How People Come to Believe They Were Kidnapped by Aliens*, Cambridge, MA: Harvard University Press, 2005.

Chapter 10: Identity Traps

1 Rebecca West: *Black Lamb and Grey Falcon, a Journey through Yugoslavia*, London: Canongate, 1942, p. 1102.

2 Rosemary Hollis: *Surviving the Story, The Narrative Trap in Israel and Palestine*, London and Swansea: Der Hawk Books, 2019, p. 175.
3 The course design was influenced by Bruno Bettelheim: *The Uses of Enchantment: The Making and Importance of Fairy Tales*, New York: Knopf, 1976.
4 Hollis, p. 48.
5 Ibid., p. 71.
6 Ibid., p. 8
7 Albert of Aachen: *History of the Journey to Jerusalem*, vol. 1: *The First Crusade, 1095–1099*, translated by Susan B. Edgington, London: Routledge, 2016, Book 5, p. 194: *It is extraordinary to relate and horrifying to the ears … the Christians did not shrink from eating not only killed Turks or Saracens, but even dogs whom they snatched and cooked with fire*; Robert the Monk: *History of the First Crusade*, translated by Carol Sweetenham, Farnham: Ashgate, 2005, p. 186: *They were so desperate with hunger that they ended up – a horrible thing to have to describe – cutting up the bodies of the Turks, cooking them and eating them*; The *Gesta Francorum* (Deeds of the Franks), in Christopher Tyerman (ed.): *Chronicles of the First Crusade*, London: Penguin Books, 2012, p. 260, also has them eating the bodies of the dead: *some of our men could not satisfy their needs, either because of the long stay or because they were so hungry … so they ripped up the bodies of the dead … and others cut the dead flesh into slices and cooked it to eat*. Raymond of Aguilers (in Tyerman, p. 269) wrote: *the food shortage became so acute that the Christians ate with gusto many rotten Saracen bodies which they had pitched into the swamps two or three weeks before*. Fulcher of Chartres (Edward Peters ed.: *The First Crusade, the Chronicle of Fulcher of Chartres and Other Source Materials*, 2nd edn, Philadelphia, PA: University of Pennsylvania Press, 1998, p. 84) wrote: *I shudder to tell that many of our people, harassed by the madness of excessive hunger, cut pieces from the buttocks of the Saracens already dead there, which they cooked … they devoured it with savage mouth.*
8 Ralph of Caen: *The* Gesta Tancredi *of Ralph of Caen, A History of the Normans on the First Crusade*, translated by Bernard S. Bachrach and David S. Bachrach, Farnham: Ashgate, 2010, chapter 97, p. 116.
9 Amin Malouf: *The Crusades through Arab Eyes*, translated by Jon Rothschild, London: Saqi Books, 1984, p. 270.
10 Ibid., pp. 39–40.

11 Albert of Aachen, Book 6, p. 224.
12 Osama bin Laden: *Messages to the World, Statements of Osama bin Laden*, edited by Bruce Lawrence. Translated by James Howarth, London: Verso, 2005, pp. 135–7.
13 Jonathan Riley-Smith: *The Crusades, a History*, 3rd edn, London: Bloomsbury, 2014, p. 340.
14 Paul M. Cobb: *The Race for Paradise, an Islamic History of the Crusades*, Oxford: Oxford University Press, 2014, pp. 177–8.
15 Osama bin Laden, p. 187.
16 Thomas Aquinas: *Letter on the Treatment of Jews*, 1271, Eighth Response, quoted in Ray Montgomery and Bob O'Dell: *The List, Persecution of Jews through History*, Hebron: Root Source Press, 2019, p. 184.
17 Montgomery and O'Dell, pp. 285–6.
18 Shakespeare: *The Merchant of Venice*, Act 3, scene 1.
19 Obituary: Anthony Meredith Quinton, London: British Academy, 2011.
20 Campion's Brag, reproduced in Evelyn Waugh: *Edmund Campion: Jesuit and Martyr*, London: Penguin Books, 1961, Appendix One.
21 Bernard Avishai: The fight to define the very essence of Israel. *Observer*, 20 May 2018.
22 John Stuart Mill: *On Liberty*, many editions, in chapter three: Of Individuality.
23 Gilles Kepel, with Antoine Jardin: *Terror in France, the Rise of Jihad in the West*, English Language edition, Princeton, NJ: Princeton University Press, 2017.
24 Ibid., p. 198.
25 This paragraph draws heavily on the *Wikipedia* account of the Enniskillen bombing.
26 https://www.erneic.org.uk/principals-welcome.
27 Abby Wallace: It's time to end school segregation, *Guardian*, 3 December 2021.
28 Quotes from Claire Bailey that follow are from Northern Ireland Council for Integrated Education: *The Big Small Stories Book: There Were No Desks*, 2018, pp. 6–8.
29 This deprivation may go far beyond politics and religion. It is often assumed that development of reasoning is internal to a person's mind. But Hugo Mercier and Dan Sperber make a good case for a more social view: *We produce reasons in order to justify our thoughts and actions to others and produce arguments to convince others to think and act as we suggest. We also use reason to evaluate not so much our own thought as the reasons others produce to justify themselves or to*

convince us. Hugo Mercier and Dan Sperber: *The Enigma of Reason, A New Theory of Human Understanding*, London: Penguin Books, 2018, p. 7. If their account is broadly right, belief-segregated education may deprive children of exercise important for developing their ability to reason.

30 Ben Winsor: Israel's Integrated Schools Provide a Vision for an Integrated Israel, p. 5. https://jstreet.org/israels -integrated-schools-provide-a-vision-for-an-integrated-israel/ #.Xnkldj7QuU. See also Yardena Schwartz: The Two School Solution, https://foreignpolicy.com/2016/05/18/the-two-school -solution-israeli-arab-children-educatioin-integration/.

31 James's phrase 'irreducible and stubborn facts' was used to characterize a key feature of modern science by A.N. Whitehead in his *Science and the Modern World*, London: Macmillan, 1925.

32 Oakeshott, p. 541.

33 Robyn Cresswell and Bernard Haykel: Poetry in Jihadi Culture, in Thomas Hegghammer (ed.): *Jihadi Culture the Art and Social Practices of Militant Islamists*, Cambridge: Cambridge University Press, 2017, p. 23.

34 Ibid., p. 28.

35 Kate Clanchy: *Some Kids I Taught and What They Taught Me*, London: Picador, 2019, p. 269.

36 Shukria Rezaei: To the Taliban, in Kate Clanchy (ed.): *England, Poems from a School*, London: Picador, 2018, p. 47.

Epilogue

1 Fernand Braudel: *The Mediterranean and the Mediterranean World in the Age of Philip II*, vol. 1, translated by Sian Reynolds, London: William Collins, 1972, p. 21.

Printed in the USA
CPSIA information can be obtained
at www.ICGtesting.com
CBHW070103010724
10714CB00006B/6/J